In the Stillness, Waiting

Christian Origins of the Prayer of the Heart

Nicholas Alan Worssam, SSF

LITURGICAL PRESS
Collegeville, Minnesota
litpress.org

Scripture quotations are from New Revised Standard Version Bible: Anglicized Edition, copyright © 1989, 1995 National Council of the Churches of Christ in the United States of America. Used by permission. All rights reserved worldwide.

Originally published in the UK under the title *In The Stillness Waiting* by the Canterbury Press, an imprint of Hymns Ancient & Modern Ltd of 13a Hellesdon Park Road, Norwich, Norfolk NR6 5DR

Printed in the United States of America.

A catalog record is available from the Library of Congress.

ISBN 979-8-4008-0231-7   979-8-4008-0232-4 (e-book)

Nicholas Worssam captures the essential elements of stillness in the development of silence and prayer as discerned in the formative Eastern classics of Christian spirituality through the centuries to this day. His emphasis on the discipline involved in acquiring 'prayer of the heart' is encapsulated in the common and universal thread of learning to sit, stop and simply wait! His interpretation of prominent representatives and key readings of this tradition—both familiar and fresh—reveals the contours of a journey in these pages that is well worth the time and effort of every traveller.

—John Chryssavgis, Professor of Theology, Holy Cross School of Theology; Executive Director, Huffington Ecumenical Institute at HCHC

This is a masterly distillation of the central teachings of the Eastern Christian tradition of prayer and discipleship. Brother Nicholas Alan provides a vivid, accessible introduction to the major texts of the 'Golden Age' of spiritual writing between the fourth and the eleventh centuries.

—Rowan Williams, former Archbishop of Canterbury

A historical account which brings alive individual personalities; a spiritual analysis which invites us to enter and participate; an objective assessment which conveys the author's personal experience—Brother Nicholas has managed to unite seemingly opposite qualities in a beautifully sensitive narrative which charts the hesychast path to union with God. This series of stepping stones provides a guide for both the complete novice and the life-long practitioner or spiritual guide. The author's Anglican background enables a refreshing interpretation of an Eastern spirituality that has recently become widely appreciated in the West as an ancient, yet also contemporary, practice within the Christian contemplative tradition.

—Mother Mary, Saint Sunniva Hermitage, Shetland Islands UK (Orthodox Church)

Amidst a frenetic and angst-ridden world, Brother Nicholas Alan SSF slows our pace to come away for a little while to a deserted place filled with the silence of prayer and the prayer of silence. This book, rooted in the rich wisdom of the Christian monastic tradition, might enable you to hear God's voice echo through the silence, and so warm your heart.

—The Rt Revd Graham Usher, Bishop of Norwich

In Chapter 6 of this book, Brother Nicholas Alan SSF states that, 'For the hesychasts, love and knowledge are intimately related.' So also for this book. Nicholas Alan has produced a work which draws deeply upon the hesychastic tradition and presents its riches in an engaging and clear-eyed fashion. While highlighting some of the tensions and dilemmas of the tradition, he moves beyond the obvious to the complexities of thinking about, for example, the body, passion and gender relationships. This is a knowledgeable book, and at times a beautiful book, which points to the destination of this tradition, and of all prayer, to the God who loves all creation beyond measure, and who invites all creation to share in the life of the divine.

—Helen Stanton, Warden of Holland House Retreat Centre, Cropthorne, Worcestershire

In this book, Nicholas Worssam reminds us that silence is more than the suppression of unnecessary or unpleasant noise: silence is a space that is ready to receive the other—and eventually welcome God's self-disclosure in Christ. This exploration of the Eastern Christian spiritual traditions maps the trajectory of desert asceticism and hesychastic spirituality from its fourth-century beginnings to its Byzantine heyday and its contemporary representatives. What we find here is an invitation to attentiveness and vigilance, and a call to a deeper integration where the mind and the heart can truly come together in prayer.

—Thomas Cattoi, Associate Professor of Christology and Cultures, Jesuit School of Theology at Santa Clara University and Graduate Theological Union, Berkeley, CA

Contents

On God alone my soul in stillness waits.
(Psalm 62:1, The Daily Office SSF)

be silent
still
aware
for there
in your own heart
the Spirit is at prayer
listen and learn
open and find
heart-wisdom
Christ

(Malling Abbey)

Acknowledgements

With grateful thanks to those who have read the manuscript of this book as it emerged and made invaluable suggestions and corrections. Particular thanks go to Mother Mary, Orthodox hermit of Saint Sunniva hermitage, Shetland Islands, UK and Revd. Canon Dr. Janet Williams, Vice Principal, St. Hild College. Many thanks also to Christine Smith and all at Canterbury Press for their encouragement and generosity, particularly Rachel Geddes, Elizabeth Hinks and Christopher Pipe who proofread my text; and also to my brothers and sisters in the Society of Saint Francis. Thanks to Father Silouan of St. David's for his penetrating gaze, to Revd. Paul Hunt to for his enthusiasm for all things Orthodox, to Revd. Andrew Mayes for his foreword to this book, and to all who read my manuscript and offered commendations.

This book is dedicated to the memory of Brother Ramon SSF, who lived as a solitary in our garden hermitage, surrounded by icons, and who taught me the Jesus Prayer.

Foreword

This substantial but accessible book introduces us to spiritual writers that shaped and clarified the hesychast tradition of prayer in the east—that is the mystical tradition of solitude and silence in which the Jesus Prayer played a key role: "This book aims to give a taste of the origins of hesychasm, in the conviction that it represents the heritage of the universal church." So although the word *hesychasm* may be unfamiliar to many, the book is concerned with the practice of developing receptive, expectant, listening prayer—which can turn out to be transformative.

Antony, Arsenius and Evagrius lead us into the silence of the desert. We learn the ascetic vocabulary of such key terms as silence, dispassion, mind and heart. A significant chapter introduces us to the little-heard voices of Syncletica and the Desert Mothers. Macarius the Great and the author of the Macarian Homilies celebrate the light of the Holy Spirit in prayer, while Mark the Ascetic and John Climacus lead us up Mount Sinai, teaching us the sequences of thought in the process of temptation, and how to break free from them. We learn about watchfulness and attentiveness from the sixth-century Elder saints of Gaza. Br. Nicholas somehow manages to unpack the very dense writings of Maximus the Confessor. He delights in the inspiration given us by Isaac of Syria and Symeon the New Theologian, together with Gregory Palamas. We receive here a clear, faithful retelling of the tradition, marked more by appreciation than by critique.

Br. Nicholas explores these sources with a gentle authority—we get the sense that he knows what he is talking about—the writers have resonated in his own experience. (This cannot be said of every contemporary spiritual writer.) He peppers sometimes rather solemn text with Franciscan humor and memorable modern phrases that immediately make sense to the reader: "long Covid of the soul"; "the sandpaper of community life to smooth off the rough edges of the psyche"; "Moderation is the only antidote [to gluttony, according to John Climacus], and that is produced in the mind, not found in the refrigerator." And more poetically: "Each thing is an individual color on the divine pallet, a unique fleeting fragrance of this flower garden earth, a never to be repeated combination of spice and seasoning in the kitchen of the banquet of heaven. Everything images God, reveals God, makes God tangible and real." In such words, Br. Nicholas relates ancient practices to contemporary experience.

This book should take its place alongside Olivier Clément's *Roots of Christian Mysticism* and Andrew Louth's *Origins of the Christian Mystical Tradition* as a textbook for students of spirituality and trainee spiritual directors—many of whom are woefully detached from the ancient wisdom, preferring the Nouwens and Rohrs of our age. Franciscans will learn much here about the hinterland to Francis' commitment to contemplative prayer. And as the last chapter reminds us, this is a living tradition of contemplative prayer, so desperately needed today by an activist Church.

Andrew D. Mayes

Introduction

Antony, Arsenius and the Stillness at the Heart of All Things

> *Love silence above everything else, for it brings you near to fruit which the tongue is too feeble to expound. First of all we force ourselves to be silent, but then from out of our silence something else is born that draws us into silence itself. May God grant you to perceive that which is born of silence! If you begin in this discipline I do not doubt how much light will dawn in you from it. After a time a certain delight is born in the heart as a result of the practice of this labor, and it forcibly draws the body on to persevere in stillness. A multitude of tears is born in us by this discipline, at the wondrous vision of certain things which the heart perceives distinctly, sometimes with pain and sometimes with wonder.*
>
> (Isaac of Syria, seventh century)[1]

I have always loved silence. Something within me responds to silence as the irresistible call of spring summons a robin to sing, or the summer sun calls me to sit in the shadow of a tree, or an autumn breeze causes me to fill my lungs with the scent of roses already beginning to fade, or the darker afternoons of winter invite me to draw the curtains, lock the door and give thanks for the passing of another day. Silence allows me to expand, to reach out to the world with less anxiety, without the fear of being overwhelmed by sound. Of course, silence in the natural world is never complete, never a total absence of noise. Silence in the countryside is a symphony of sound—the song of a blackbird, the susurration of a poplar avenue, the barking of deer, the patter of rain, distant voices carried on the wind. Even "man-made" sounds, like the passing of a train on a far-off track, or cars on an unseen road, or the breath of fire blowing into a hot-air balloon overhead like a whale surfacing to take a deep breath, all these sounds can take me out of myself, into the intricate network of society, the world of people I will hear just this once, and probably never see or hear again. In the thousand-fold sounds of silence I find myself to be part of a web of relationships, an infinity of connections, billions of ways of being myself in the company of others. The connectivity of silence helps me to open my heart to others, to realize that we are all in this together, whatever this particular moment, this particular pattern of inter-connectivity may bring.

And it seems to me that this is a large part of what it means to pray—to realize that I am not alone and never could be, to become a part of the divine life, an in-breath and out-breath of the Holy Spirit of God, a silent holding of the hand of God. It is in silence that I most come alive and am able to share that life with others, just to be with a beloved friend without the need to speak in words, enough just to be and be happy, here and now. Silence can, of course, be stifling, if it is imposed on ourselves or on others whom we love. The refusal to listen to another, not to allow them to move in to and out of silence, is a form of violence, no matter how little physical contact there may be. This is not true silence. This is the imposition of noise—an anti-silence, a white noise that drowns out everything other than itself. True silence allows compassion to take root, awareness to flourish, and joy to sink into our bones. "Love silence above everything else," says St. Isaac the Syrian, "for it brings you near to fruit which the tongue is too feeble to expound." And he's right—love silence and silence will echo that love, filling you with joy and peace in believing.

Silence is a discipline, a skill to be learned with patient endurance. It requires that we unlearn our habitual dependencies—the automatic turning on of the news, the constant checking of emails, the glance at the phone for messages that prolong an inconsequential conversation. It is the resolution to deny just a little of the data that feeds the hungry world wide web, to insist on limits to being on call. But such abstinence, no matter how insignificant it may seem, might just be the beginning of another way of being with others, another expression of kindness. And in the process there may be tears, as we learn the art of love once again, as we allow ourselves to be open to the pain and joy of others, and to recognize our own.

This is a book about silence. Already it is a contradiction. How can we speak of silence? More to the point, how can we speak of that which is beyond expression, to hint at the One who dwells in a "Cloud of Unknowing" as described in a fourteenth-century English manual of prayer? It has been the conviction of those drawn to the practice of silent contemplation that there are things that can only be communicated silently, or breathed quietly in the stillness of prayer. In particular there is a tradition within the church known as "hesychasm," from the Greek word "*hesychia*" (*ἡσυχία*), meaning stillness or silence.

There are many written teachings, both in the Eastern and Western traditions of Christianity, to help those who wish to pursue this practice of silence. This book will explore some of the more central texts, mostly from the Coptic, Greek and Syriac traditions, as treasured by the churches of Egypt, Palestine, Syria and Byzantium. Further developments came as Christianity spread to Eastern Europe and beyond, but these are outside the scope of this short book, which will focus particularly on the Greek tradition.

There are a number of technical terms that cluster around the central Greek concept of *hesychia*, and it will help to begin by getting a general overview of how these terms overlap and relate to each other. Chief among these terms are "the guarding of the heart" or "watchfulness," which leads to the descent of the "mind" into the "heart," that enables "pure, imageless prayer."

Coming to terms with silence

The editors of the English translation of *The Philokalia*, a classic compendium of texts on hesychastic prayer, define "*hesychia*," the practice of silence, as:

> A state of inner tranquillity or mental quietude and concentration which arises in conjunction with, and is deepened by, the practice of pure prayer and the guarding of the heart and intellect. Not

> simply silence, but an attitude of listening to God and of openness towards Him.[2]

"Pure prayer" is prayer that has gone beyond concepts of God; it does not seek to define God or limit God in any way. It is related to "the guarding of the heart and intellect," otherwise known as "watchfulness" (Greek: *νῆψις/nepsis*).[3] This watchfulness is the attitude of attentiveness, keeping watch over the thoughts and emotions that inhabit the heart. "Pure prayer" is an active listening to God, the enjoyment of a stillness that descends on the one who prays after thoughts have been let go, a tuning of the ear to the presence of God in the "sound of sheer silence" (1 Kings 19:12) as heard by Elijah on Mount Horeb.

More particularly, "pure prayer" is the cleansing of the intellect or mind (*νοῦς/nous*), a word used in this tradition not of the rational mind or deductive reasoning, but of direct apprehension or spiritual perception, our ability to recognize truth when we see it. Rowan Williams uncovers some of the meaning of the term "*nous*":

> *Nous* is that capacity at the very centre of our being for turning Godwards, since God is what is unconditionally real. So when *nous* is identified, as it often is in Greek Christian literature, with the 'image of God' in us, this doesn't mean that God's image is in the mind rather than the body, or anything like that; it is simply saying that the centre of everything that we are as finite human subjects is this 'magnetic' turning in the direction of God—the iron filings twitching at the approach of the magnet.[4]

"*Nous*" is a word still current in the English language, meaning something like "practical intelligence" or simply "common sense" and, in a more technically philosophical sense, referring to the intellect. In its spiritual sense, however, as used in the hesychastic tradition, the *nous* enables an immediate insight into the nature of reality, and is defined in the sixth-century *Macarian Homilies* as "the eye of the heart."

In the hesychast spiritual tradition in general, the word "heart" itself has a very particular meaning, as Kallistos Ware explains:

> When they speak about the word heart (*καρδία/kardia*), they understand the word in its Semitic and Biblical sense, as signifying not just the emotions and affections but the primary centre of our human personhood. The heart signifies the deep self; it is the seat of wisdom and understanding, the place where our moral decisions are made, the inner shrine in which we experience divine grace and the indwelling presence of the Holy Trinity. It indicates the human person as a 'spiritual subject,' created in God's image and likeness.[5]

The heart is the place in which we rest in the presence of God, and also the arena into which we lead the mind as we struggle to open the heart to God. It is not the place of romantic dreams, though all the energy of love is expended in its opening to the beloved Lord.

Hesychasm is thus a response to the scriptural teaching of Proverbs 4:23: "Keep your heart with all vigilance, for from it flow the springs of life." Be aware of the state of your heart, the hesychasts tell us, because it is there that the irrepressible life of Christ is to be found, an energy which can be used for good or for ill. This is at one and the same time a work of utmost seriousness and exertion, as well as a celebration of the presence of the Lord who himself guards the heart and drives away all fear, "[for] the peace of God, which surpasses all understanding, will guard your hearts and your minds in Christ Jesus" (Phil 4:7).

When the mind descends into the heart in this way, then it is known in this tradition as "the prayer of the heart." Again, Kallistos Ware explains the significance of this term:

> When our prayer becomes, in the fullest sense, 'prayer of the heart', we have already approached the threshold of unceasing prayer . . . True prayer of the heart is no longer just something that we recite, but it is part of ourselves, just as the drawing of breath or the beating of our heart is part of ourselves. And so by God's grace the prayer comes to be, no longer something that a person has to say, but something that says itself within him.[6]

Although in this tradition some of the key terms have a degree of fluidity of meaning, there are arguably two main strands of this practice of prayer. The first is the watchfulness that guards the mind, recognizing patterns of afflictive thought, and substituting virtues for vice. The second is described as "the descent of the mind into the heart"; that is, the deep enjoyment of a mind finally at rest, the transformation of the energy of thoughts and feelings into the radiant goodness of a person full of the divine compassion in the "pure prayer" beyond conceptual thinking. These two strands I have alluded to in the title and subtitle of this book. "In the Stillness, Waiting" refers to the stillness that leads to watchfulness, waiting with joyful expectancy for the revelation of the presence of God, and "the prayer of the heart," points to the eventual transformation of bodies and souls in the ceaseless contemplation of God, becoming one with God with all our heart and mind.

This book aims to give a taste of the origins of hesychasm, in the conviction that it represents the heritage of the universal church. This wisdom belongs to all Christians, even though it has been faithfully handed on especially by the Orthodox Church over the last 2,000 years. All the authors quoted here, apart from the final chapter, come from the time before the official split between the Western Catholic and Eastern Orthodox churches, nominally dated as occurring in 1054. In the final chapter we look at two slightly later authors who have helped to give hesychasm its classic definition, Symeon the New Theologian and Gregory Palamas. In the Postscript we look at the twentieth century, showing that this is a living tradition, still exemplified by teachers of hesychastic prayer in the modern world. These descriptions summarize a tradition going back to the very beginnings of the Christian church, to the teaching of Jesus Christ and the Apostle Paul.

Companions on the Way

Hesychasm is rooted in the experience of the women and men who withdrew from the cities of the Roman empire in the third and fourth centuries of the Common Era, and established communities of renunciates in the deserts of Egypt. There were always both women and men committed to this pursuit, but the women spoke more quietly than the men, or were not listened to by the men, and their wisdom was rarely recorded. All were "monks," a word deriving from the Greek word "*monos*" (*μόνος*), meaning "one" or "solitary," though the term came to be applied solely to men. The monk was one who delighted in solitude and silence because they enabled the noise of the mind to be more closely analyzed and the "passions" stilled. Through such an unflinching knowledge of the self, unhelpful patterns of thought could be unraveled and discarded, with new connections made in their place. Silence became an uninscribed book, or tablet, on which to write the words of revelation whispered in the ear by the Spirit of discernment and understanding. It provided a blank page, a *tabula rasa*, on which to recount this voyage of discovery.

All this applies to women just as much as men. The word "nun" doesn't have the same connotations, being derived from the late Latin word "*nonna*," meaning "tutor," or just being a term of endearment and respect for an elder, like "nana" in modern English. But there were, and are, respected female elders in this tradition, as will be seen in a later chapter. It is to be hoped that their voices will be more clearly heard in times to come.

The designation "monk" has a further meaning to do with corporate unity. As Evagrius of Pontus (345–399) says: "A monk is one who is separated from all and who is in harmony with all. A monk is one who considers himself [herself] one with all people because [they] seem constantly to see [themselves] in everyone."[7] To understand oneself is to understand all people, not because all are identical carbon copies, but because each one reflects the image of God—Christ, the archetype of humanity. Christ indwells all people, holding them in being (Col 1:17), revealing their essential unity in the love of God.

Augustine of Hippo (354–430), north African theologian and bishop, emphasized this communal dimension of being at one with others. He wrote in his commentary on the Psalm text: "How very good and pleasant it is when kindred live together in unity!" (Ps 133:1):

> Those who live in unity in such a way that they form but one person are rightly called '*monos*', one single person. They make true to life what is written, 'of one mind and one heart', that is, many bodies but not many hearts.[8]

Today those who choose celibacy as a tool for this art of contemplative prayer can be called "monastics" or "religious," making nouns out of adjectives to achieve a more inclusive expression. But this kind of prayer is not a practice for monastic celibates alone. It is the universal human calling. In essence it is the calling to love. The hesychasts practiced watchfulness, the guarding of the heart, because it led to *apatheia*, or "dispassion," which in turn was found to be a help towards enabling them to love. As we shall see in Chapter 1, Evagrius outlines a basic progression in the spiritual life from dispassion (*ἀπάθεια/apatheia*) to love (*ἀγάπη/agape*) to knowledge (*γνῶσις/gnosis*) of God. *Apatheia*, while seen as a central value in this tradition, is one of the hardest virtues to come to terms with in our own day. It is most definitely not the same thing as the modern English word "apathy," despite their etymological similarity.

The translators of *The Philokalia* offer a succinct definition:

> Dispassion is a state of reintegration and spiritual freedom; when translating the term into Latin, Cassian [a disciple of Evagrius] rendered it 'purity of heart'. Such a state may imply impartiality and detachment, but not indifference, for [even] if a dispassionate man does not suffer on his own account, he suffers for his fellow creatures.[9]

True dispassion is about discovering the liberating power of silence, the still mind that enables the individual to welcome into their lives those whom God calls them to love. The paradox is that solitude lived well brings out the closeness that always exists between members of the body of Christ; and who is not a member, ultimately, of the body of the One who fills all things? (See Eph 1:22-23.) A practitioner of silent prayer aims to know the one thing necessary (Luke 10:42) rather than the many things possible, the pearl of great price (Matt 13:46) rather than the bargain of the moment, the eye made single and clear and bright (Matt 6:22), so that they may see with greater clarity the image of God in the person in whose presence they are called to live.

Antony the Great and the call to solitude

Chief among these early Christian hesychasts was Antony (251–356), known subsequently as "Antony the Great," and made famous by his eloquent biographer Athanasius (296–373), Bishop of Alexandria. In the *Life of Antony*, one of the first examples of Christian hagiography, Athanasius tells the story of how one day in church, Antony heard the Gospel reading about the rich young man, who was told by Jesus: "If you wish to be perfect, go, sell your possessions, and give the money to the poor, and you will have treasure in heaven; then come, follow me" (Matt 19:21). This message resonated with his whole being, so he fulfilled the commandment to the letter, distributed his goods to the poor, and dedicated himself to Christ. Having left his home and made arrangements for the care of his sister, Antony went to learn the ways of prayer from another monk already established at the edge of a nearby town. For 15 years, at first in the company of his monastic guide, and then in greater seclusion in an abandoned tomb, Antony lived an austere ascetic life, sleeping little and surviving on a diet of bread, salt and water. He was plagued by visions of demons and fierce beasts, perhaps due to the hieroglyphics on the walls of his dwelling swarming towards him in terrifying hallucinations. Later, he felt called to go ever deeper into the solitude and silence of the Egyptian desert, and for a further 20 years lived in an abandoned fort, seeing no one, but receiving food and water from a dedicated disciple. Eventually Antony opened the door and stepped out into the crowds now gathered outside his hermitage. He was not emaciated and crazed as might have been expected, but in complete sanity and health of body and mind, encouraging the people by his words and healing the sick. Does this mean that all Christians intent on finding God should sell all their possessions and head for the nearest wilderness? Are all called to be solitaries in the desert? Antony advises otherwise:

> There are some who've worn out their bodies doing ascetic practices, and because of this, they've lost the power of discernment and have become far from God.
> (He also said) I know monks who, after great exertions, fell and lost their minds because they put their trust in their own work and didn't consider the commandment that says, 'Ask your father, and he will inform you' (Deut. 32.7).[10]

It was all a question of balance, and discernment of what was the right thing to do at any given time. Don't get carried away, says the wise Antony, the body should be treated with respect. Pride is always lurking at the door, and vainglory is the final arrow fired by the enemy at a seemingly triumphant monk or nun. Know your limits and take every step forward as a gift of grace: this is the teaching of Antony.

But a key part of the advice he gleans from the Scriptures is to "ask your father," that is, to seek the counsel of a wise spiritual guide. Antony went alone into the desert, but that was something of an anomaly. Most desert monastics went into the wilderness to join with a small group, each of them unburdening themselves of their thoughts to a resident elder who had himself or herself sat at the feet of a wise guide. Complete solitude is rarely the cure for a troubled mind but, in the presence of a wise father or mother (in Greek: *abba* or *amma*) to ask for advice, the possibility of inner healing is greatly increased.

With the aid of a spiritual guide, the disciple's thoughts were revealed in the stillness of the desert; outer quietness became at first an amplifier of inner turmoil, and only later was there the possibility of a continuing harmonization of outer and inner silence in a resonant stillness of the heart. Included in a record of Antony's sayings is the enigmatic advice:

> He who sits alone and is quiet has escaped from three wars: hearing, speaking, seeing: but there is one thing against which he must continually fight: that is, his own heart.[11]

Antony was like a soldier giving all his attention to the battle at hand, knowing that if he lost concentration for a moment his life would be at risk, bearing the armor and weapons of a spiritual warrior as described by St. Paul (see Eph 6:10-17). His enemies were not other people but his own afflictive desires. In later chapters we will explore in greater detail the classifications of such thoughts, their causes, and the sequences in which they often approach the unwary soul. Evagrius and John Climacus were particularly concerned to clarify these matters, and so aid those on the arduous climb up the spiritual ladder to the nearer presence of God, as we will see in more detail in later chapters. In the quote above the three wars are hearing, speaking and seeing, suggesting a general need for solitude and quiet as a basis for prayer. For some, the continuous fight against the heart was primarily to do with loneliness and desire—the hearing of a longed-for voice, the whispered invitation to a secret tryst, and the sight of the one beloved. Nonetheless, the heart, the arena within which Antony fought, was seen in those days as the repository of all the thoughts, crowded out by all kinds of desires, hatreds and confusions that befog the mind. It was sometimes said by the desert elders that the struggle against anger was the hardest battle to fight—love and desire merely had to be redirected towards their proper object, that is, God. Nevertheless, in whichever order the thoughts fight against us, the pure heart is free of both attraction and repulsion, free to love without clinging, and full of vigor without hate.

But what exactly do the desert elders mean when they talk about the pure heart? Purity of heart is to see God, says Jesus in Matthew's Gospel (5:8), but that purity is discovered in the abandonment of the supposedly separate self, and the discovery of the self that sees with God's eyes, always and only in love. Gradually, over 35 years, Anthony had won the battle against distraction and delusion, and by the grace of God emerged with a clear mind and a pure heart, completely human, honed by the stillness and silence of the desert.

Teaching from the heart

It was not just clarity of mind that Antony discovered in the desert, it was compassion that was the immediate consequence of inner stillness of the heart. It seems that love naturally welled up in

Antony as an instinctive response to the overwhelming knowledge that he was loved by God, that God was always with him regardless of how far away from God he might have felt in the inner turmoil of his early years in solitude.

Another story about Antony reveals the universality of his teaching, and the simple human kindness that he showed to those in his care:

> There was a certain man, a hunter, who hunted wild animals throughout the wilderness region, and he saw Abba Antony laughing and joking with the brothers and was scandalized.
>
> The elder [Antony], wanting to assure him, because he needed to accommodate himself from time to time to the level of the brothers, said to him, 'Put an arrow in your bow and stretch the bow tight,' and this he did.
>
> Antony said to him, 'Stretch it tight some more,' and he stretched it some more.
>
> Again he said, 'Stretch it.'
>
> The hunter said to him, 'If I stretch it too tight, the bow will break.'
>
> The elder said to him, 'It's the same with doing God's work: with regard to the brothers, if we stretch them too tight, they'll quickly break into pieces. It's necessary, then, to come down to the brothers' level from time to time.'
>
> When the hunter heard what Antony was saying, he was deeply moved and, having benefited greatly from the elder, departed. The brothers, strengthened and feeling supported, withdrew to their monastic settlement.[12]

Mutual support and understanding are essential for this practice. Despite the depictions of almost incredible austerities, the more important values of kindness and discernment take precedence. Prudence is one of the great virtues of the monastic life, and without it the aspirant is heading for a fall.

Another of Antony's sayings brings out the simple joy that others found in his presence:

> Three of the fathers had the custom to go see the blessed Antony each year. Two of them would ask him about their thoughts and the salvation of their souls, but the one always remained silent and wouldn't ask anything. Quite a while later, Abba Antony said to him, 'Look, you've been coming here all this time, and you never ask me anything.' He responded, saying to him, 'It's enough for me just to see you, father.'[13]

Spiritual guidance is not always by words—a warm welcome, a look of compassion, and a quiet listening ear are sometimes all that is needed for a heart to be put at rest. But the seeing is still important. Seeing in memory or hearing from others or from a book won't satisfy a truly earnest soul—the proximity of flesh and blood is what remolds the body and retunes the soul in need of reformation.

One final story about Abba Antony, from the thematic collection of sayings and stories from the desert elders, shows the reputation of this remarkable human being:

> A brother asked an elder, 'What can I do, father? I'm not doing anything befitting a monk; instead, I'm indifferent and neglectful—I eat and drink and sleep; I'm prone to shameful thoughts, and I'm very upset, very unsettled, moving from one thing to another and from one thought to the next.'
>
> The elder said, 'Sit in your cell, and whatever you're able to do, do, without getting upset about it. Here's what I think: the little bit that you do now is like the great works that Abba Antony used to do in the desert, and it's my belief that the person who sits in his own cell for the sake of the name of God and keeps watch over his conscience—that person, too, will be found where Abba Antony is.'[14]

Or as another of the first generation of monks, Moses the Egyptian, famously said: "Go and sit in your cell, and your cell will teach you everything."[15] The cell of the monastic is not a prison but a furnace, a place to purify the precious mind and pour away the dross. The true cell is of course the heart, the "inner room" spoken of by Jesus as the place from which to pray to the Father who hears and dwells in secret (Matt 6:6). It is a pillar of cloud by day and a pillar of fire by night, guiding out of captivity the one who dwells within. The conversion of the soul in its cell is the exodus from Egypt to the promised land, the land flowing with milk and honey, the mind set free and nourished on the sweetness of truth. "Your commandments are sweeter than honey to my mouth," says the psalmist (Ps 19:7-10). To savor those crisp honeycombs is to know the delight of the knowledge of God: the dispassionate longing for God fulfilled, the all-consuming desire for the Eternal satisfied in time.

Arsenius and the silence of the desert

Soon after Antony, another great hero of this way of life emerged to prominence in the desert. This was Arsenius (c. 360–c. 449), once tutor to the emperor's children, but then called by an internal voice to abandon the Roman court life and flee:

> Abba Arsenius, when he was still at the palace, prayed to God, saying, 'Lord, guide me: How can I be saved?' A voice came to him saying, 'Arsenius, flee people, and you will be saved.' The same Arsenius, after he had withdrawn from the world to live as a solitary, prayed once again, asking the same question, and he heard a voice saying to him, 'Arsenius, flee, maintain silence, live a life of contemplative quiet. These are the roots of being without sin.'[16]

"Flee, be silent, pray always." These were the three mandates that transformed his life. Giving up the luxury of the palace he embraced the poverty of the desert, and wept for the lost years behind him. It was said that in the evening on Saturdays he would stand to pray facing west, watching the sun go down in front of him. Then, as the stars began to shine as if willing him to silently navigate by night, he would turn to the east and pray to the risen Son until the rising sun brought with it a brief time of rest.[17]

But such solitude was not, and is not, the path of all people. Amma Syncletica knew that well:

> There are many who live in the mountains and behave as if they were in the town, and they are wasting their time. It is possible to be a solitary in one's mind while living in a crowd, and it is possible for one who is a solitary to live in the crowd of his own thoughts.[18]

Outer and inner solitude do not always come together. Each can be a torment in its own way. The delight of aloneness can all too easily become the despair of loneliness; the hermitage can be noisier than a crowd. Better to seek peace in the city than to be tormented by the terrifying silence of the wilderness. But where can the peace of silence be found?

> A brother asked Abba Rufus, 'What is interior peace, and what use is it?' The old man said, 'Interior peace means to remain sitting in one's cell with fear and knowledge of God, holding far off the remembrance of wrongs suffered and pride of spirit. Such interior peace brings forth all the virtues, preserves the monk from the burning darts of the enemy, and does not allow him to be wounded by them. Yes, brother, acquire it. Keep in mind your future death, remembering that you do not know at what hour the thief will come. Likewise be watchful over your soul.'[19]

True solitude entails the letting go of "I, me, mine," not just in the outward circumstances of life but by the inward inclination of the mind. Here all grudges can finally be let go, all toxic memories of wrongs suffered be allowed to blow away as dust in the wind. Ashes to ashes, dust to dust, all that we cling to dies, while all that we relinquish for the sake of God's kingdom is returned to us for good. The letting go is the precursor to receiving a hundredfold, and is accomplished by the simple, and extraordinarily difficult, practice of watchfulness—waiting for the Lord to return, being prepared with lamps lit in prayer, and looking for the one who comes when we least expect. Above all, watch, wait, and be ready to act with the calm intuitive wisdom of a mind still and refreshed. Then there is hope that our actions will be appropriate to the given task, and our hearts will be open to all the beauty and wonder of this world.

> This story was told: There were three friends, serious men, who became monks. One of them chose to make peace between men who were at odds, as it is written, "Blessed are the peacemakers" (Matt 5:9). The second chose to visit the sick. The third chose to go away to be quiet in solitude. Now the first, toiling among contentions, was not able to settle all quarrels and, overcome with weariness, he went to him who tended the sick and found him also failing in spirit and unable to carry out his purpose. So the two went away to see him who had withdrawn into the desert, and they told him their troubles. They asked him to tell them how he himself had fared. He was silent for a while, and then poured water into a vessel and said, "Look at the water," and it was murky. After a little while he said again, "See now, how clear the water has become." As they looked into the water they saw their own faces, as in a mirror. Then he said to them, "So it is with anyone who lives in a crowd; because of the turbulence, he does not see his sins: but when he has been quiet, above all in solitude, then he recognizes his own faults."[20]

The recognition of faults in quiet and solitude, which leads to the gift of tears, is not ultimately a sorrowful journey. In the morning the joy of God's name is finally revealed:

> Sing praises to the Lord, O you his faithful ones,
> and give thanks to his holy name . . .
> Weeping may linger for the night,
> but joy comes with the morning. (Ps 30:4-5)

I commend to you this practice of *hesychia*, this stillness, silence and radiant well-being, to be perfected by the grace of God over a lifetime and beyond. May it be a source of abundant joy.

Questions for reflection and discussion

- Do you pray more with your heart or with your head? Is there a difference?
- Do you find silence helpful, or even possible, in prayer?

- Where do you go to find peace and quiet in your life?

Further reading

Benedicta Ward SLG, 2003, *The Desert Fathers: Sayings of the Early Christian Monks* [the Thematic Collection], London: Penguin Books.
John Chryssavgis, 2003, *In the Heart of the Desert: The Spirituality of the Desert Fathers and Mothers*, Bloomington, IN: World Wisdom.
Rowan Williams, 2004, *Silence and Honey Cakes: The Wisdom of the Desert*, London: Lion Books.

Notes

1 Sebastian Brock (trans.) and A. M. Allchin (ed.), 1989, *Heart of Compassion: Daily Readings with St. Isaac of Syria*, London: Darton, Longman & Todd, p. 22.

2 G. E. H. Palmer, Philip Sherrard and Kallistos Ware, 1979, 1981, 1984, 1995, 2023, *The Philokalia: The Complete Text, compiled by St Nikodimos of the Holy Mountain and St Makarios of Corinth*, Five Volumes, Londer: Faber, vol. 1, p. 364.

3 All translations of technical terms are from the Greek. However, the spelling of Greek names follows the Latinate style more familiar in the Western Church, hence: John Climacus rather than John Klimakos.

4 Rowan Williams, 2024, *Passions of the Soul*, London: Bloomsbury Continuum, pp. xx–xxi.

5 Bishop Kallistos Ware, 2001, *The Inner Kingdom, Volume 1 of the Collected Works*, New York: St Vladimir's Seminary Press, pp. 61–2.

6 Ware, *Inner Kingdom*, pp. 82–3.

7 *Prayer* 122–125; John Eudes Bamberger OCSO, 1981, *Evagrius Ponticus: The Praktikos & Chapters on Prayer*, Collegeville, MN: Cistercian Publications, pp. 75–6.

8 Tarsicius J. Van Bavel OSA and Raymond Canning OSA, 1984, *The Rule of Saint Augustine*, London: Darton, Longman & Todd, p. 45.

9 Palmer et al, *The Philokalia*, vol. 1, p. 359.

10 Tim Vivian, 2021, *The Sayings and Stories of the Desert Fathers and Mothers, volume 1*, Collegeville, MN: Cistercian Publications, pp. 97, 115.

11 Benedicta Ward SLG, 2003, *The Desert Fathers: Sayings of the Early Christian Monks*, London: Penguin Books, p. 8.

12 Vivian, *Sayings and Stories*, pp. 100–1.

13 Vivian, *Sayings and Stories*, p. 109.

14 Vivian, *Sayings and Stories*, pp. 117–18.

15 Ward, *Desert Fathers*, p. 10.

16 Vivian, *Sayings and Stories*, pp. 119–20.

17 Vivian, *Sayings and Stories*, pp. 132–3.

18 Benedicta Ward SLG, 1975/1984 revd edn, *The Sayings of the Desert Fathers: The Alphabetical Collection*, Collegeville, MN: Cistercian Publications, p. 234.

19 Ward, *Alphabetical Collection*, p. 210.

20 Ward, *Desert Fathers*, p. 11.

1

Evagrius Ponticus and the Analysis of Dispassion

Celebrity autobiographies tend to be stories of "rags to riches"—showing how people manage to overcome desperate situations to emerge rich and famous, not least because of the ghost-writers who skillfully mold their story according to public taste. The life of Evagrius Ponticus (345–399) is more a story of riches to rags, of ecclesiastical power to monastic obscurity, of amorous liaisons to chaste celibacy, and of theological authority to heretical condemnation. In his own day he was in fact quite well known among those who looked to the desert monastics for inspiration, but he became suspect because of his connections with the early church theologian and Scripture scholar Origen of Alexandria (c. 185–c. 253). Although the views of both Origen and Evagrius were condemned at the Fifth Ecumenical Council of 553, many of the works of Evagrius survived largely under the safety of inoffensive pseudonyms, or as translations gathering dust in the forbidden sections of remote monastic libraries. Even though his name has until recently been little known, his influence has been enormous. Through his disciple John Cassian (360–435), his teaching spread to the Christian West; and in the East, under the name "Nilus," his practical works on prayer and contemplation survived the condemnation of his more speculative theological works, and guided generations of people of prayer. Above all, his influence echoes through the writings of Diodochus of Photike, John Climacus and Isaac the Syrian among others, all luminaries to be discovered and celebrated in later chapters of this book.

Palladius, in his *Lausiac History* written about the year 420, devotes a chapter to "the famous deacon Evagrius, a man who lived in truly apostolic fashion."[1] Palladius knew him well, having been his companion and disciple for nine years. Born in 345 in Pontus, now in northern Turkey, Evagrius was the son of a country bishop, and a man of great ambitions. He made his name by association with the renowned theologians known to us as the Cappadocian Fathers. Gregory of Nyssa inspired his theological writings; Basil the Great, Bishop of Caesarea, ordained him lector; and, after Basil's death his friend Gregory of Nazianzus took Evagrius under his wing, ordaining him deacon. As Archbishop of Constantinople, Gregory Nazianzus employed the young man's considerable theological and oratorical skills in the defense of what was emerging as the orthodox faith, as proclaimed at the Council of Nicaea in the year 325.

Palladius tells us that Evagrius "flourished in the great city, confuting every heresy with youthful exuberance." He was the man to know, invited to dine in the homes of the rich, and preaching at the churches of the elite. But then something happened that changed his life for ever. While cutting a dashing figure as a leading churchman of the capital of the Eastern Roman empire, his world suddenly fell apart. He fell in love with the wife of an important official, a woman of the highest social class, even though, having been ordained, he would have been expected to remain celibate. Evagrius wanted to break off the relationship to save his reputation, but was too far gone in his emotional turmoil to come to a resolution. The woman shared his feelings and by now both were "eager and frantic" for the other.

At this point Evagrius had a dream or a kind of half-waking vision. In his dream, soldiers of the governor arrested him, bound him with chains and imprisoned him in a dungeon. His fevered mind was playing out his fears, all because of his disastrous infatuation. The dream continued with an angel warning him to leave the city of Constantinople as soon as possible, saying that his life was in danger. The angel even brought a book of the Gospels on which Evagrius swore to leave immediately, or at least after taking a day to pack his bags. At this stage in his life he didn't travel light. Although this vivid scene was only a dream, Evagrius decided on waking that an oath was an oath and should be upheld. Having packed his books and his clothes, he rushed to the port and took the first boat he could find bound for Jerusalem.

Once there he took refuge with a highly respected widow and scholar, the Roman lady Melania the Elder. Melania had used her considerable financial wealth to found a convent for religious women on the Mount of Olives. There, together with a monastic friend named Rufinus, she lived a life of quiet study and prayer. Evagrius might have been expected to join them in their religious seclusion, but he still hadn't experienced a real conversion of the heart. He lived a dissipated life, wandering the streets of Jerusalem in search of good conversation and intellectual stimulation. He told his gracious hosts nothing of the reasons for his abrupt appearance in their lives. At this point his body gave way, perhaps a result of nervous exhaustion, and he became ill to the point of death, suffering from a fever for six months.

Eventually he poured out his soul to his patron Melania, who clothed him with a set of monastic robes, and encouraged him to travel to Egypt to learn from the monks the true nature of the heart and soul. Evagrius heeded her advice and left Jerusalem for a life of prayer and reclusion under the guidance of the holy ascetics known as Macarius of Egypt and Macarius the Great. There he stayed for the rest of his life, moving only a short distance after two years to a place of greater solitude and peace. Although he lived a life of internal quiet (Greek: *ἡσυχία/ hesychia*), externally he became something of a celebrity, having become a part of the spiritual tourist circuit for the devout and the curious.

The weekly routine of those gathered around him consisted of prayer, study and work in solitude during the week, and then meeting together on Saturdays and Sundays, discussing the interpretation of Scripture and the vagaries of the mind till sunrise. More difficult or personal matters he would counsel one-to-one, showing a humility and tender-heartedness, as well as a rigorously analytical mind. Unlike the other monks who earned their living by weaving rope and baskets made from reeds, Evagrius supported himself by copying manuscripts with his elegant handwriting in the Oxyrhynchus style. Every day half a dozen guests and visitors came to him for a word of wisdom to guide them on their way. He died at the age of 54, probably a result of his severely ascetic life since his flight to Egypt, and having eaten nothing but dry bread and uncooked vegetables, drinking only a little water, and sleeping just a few hours each night.

Talking Back

Evagrius, a contemporary of the famous North African bishop Augustine of Hippo (354–430), was in some ways the Augustine of the East. Both men gave up glittering careers as orators, and both wrote voluminously about the spiritual life, albeit one in Greek and the other in Latin. But Evagrius disappeared in the records of Christian history because of his speculative theology concerning the beginning and end of all things. Following his spiritual mentor Origen, Evagrius taught that there were two creation events and two falls: first, the creation of the angelic beings, and second the creation of humanity and the rest of the embodied universe. In short, souls fell into bodies, and all would eventually be liberated from their embodied selves by the grace of God and by contemplating God in the beauties of creation. Evagrian teachings that were seen as particularly in error according to Jerome and others were, for example: "that there are a plurality of worlds, some preceding this one, others to follow; that hellfire is not physical, but psychological, the burning stings of conscience; that there will be a transmigration of souls."[2] The technicalities of the debates are not easy to follow, but later condemnations led to the destruction of many of his writings, with some manuscripts surviving in translation in Syriac and Armenian, or accredited to other writers considered orthodox by the ecumenical councils of the church.

Augustine's most famous work was his *Confessions*—a blend of autobiography and complex religious philosophy. These musings give a fascinating insight into the workings of Augustine's mind, making him seem like a man of our own age. Evagrius wrote his own "confessions" in a work entitled *Antirrhetikos*, or *Talking Back*, a kind of manual or handbook for those being tempted by the devil. It consists of a list of temptations, which can lead to habitual modes of thought (*λογίσμοι/ logismoi*), together with a corresponding quotation from Scripture to rebuff each assault of the devil. Although some chapters are universal in their application, others clearly emerge directly from Evagrius' own experience. As such they give a startling insight into his way of thinking, and the solace he found both in evaluating the thoughts that plagued him, and in providing a way of reconstructing his consciousness through meditating on the words of Scripture. They throw light on a scholarly life deeply embedded in the Bible, quoting a great array of scriptural sources, and following the example of Jesus in his response to being tempted in the wilderness, as recounted by the Gospels of Matthew and Luke. Written as a manual for his brothers, *Talking Back* shows a close and unflinching observation of human nature in himself and others.

Some of the chapters are painfully heartfelt. In the chapter entitled "Against the Thoughts of Fornication" (*πορνεία/porneía*) we hear the plaintive echoes of his own love affair in Constantinople:

> Against the thoughts that compel us to linger in conversation with a married woman on the pretext that she has visited us frequently or that she will benefit spiritually from us:
> *Do not be long with someone else's woman (Prov. 5.20).*[3]

"How did I get myself into this mess?" he seems to be asking himself. "Was I fooling myself all along?" Already he is revealing how thoughts seem to compel us towards doing what we resist, an experience echoed by St. Paul in Romans 7, and clarified for many today by the insights of psychoanalysis and Cognitive Behavioral Therapy. Here in the writings of Evagrius the thoughts are already slipping their mask—thoughts are not what they seem. Arrayed against us, they are discovered to be not ourselves, but only temporary guests of the mind, whether actively welcomed or not.

In his book *Praktikos*, on the practical foundations of prayer, Evagrius explores the nature of the thoughts that he experienced, and how one thing leads to another.

Passion

> Whatever a man loves he will desire with all his might. What he desires he strives to lay hold of. Now desire precedes every pleasure,

> and it is feeling which gives birth to desire. For that which is not subject to feeling is also free of passion.[4]

Here Evagrius is examining the steps of the process of temptation (*πειρασμός/peirasmos*): the sequence of sensations or feelings of attraction, leading to desire, then pleasure, and finally the entrainment, the captivity, of passion (*πάθος/pathos*). The latter has become a technical term in this kind of ascetic discourse, and it is important to be aware of the nuances of the term "passion," and how its usage subtly differs in Greek and English. In the Greek (and Syriac) texts of the early church monastics, "passions" are any type of thinking that entrain us, take control and lead us astray. They are a kind of addiction, a desire or hatred that has become out of control and distorts perceptions, a sickness that needs healing. In modern English, however, "passion" is a positive term, suggesting vigor, energy and commitment: to be passionate for justice, peace and the well-being of creation is seen as invaluable for an integrated and healthy spiritual life. For Evagrius, and those in the battle for stillness of mind in prayer, *pathos* (passion), in the particular sense in which they used the term, was a hindrance. For these desert fathers and mothers the opposite of "passion" was dispassion or equanimity. In Greek the word is "*apatheia*" (*ἀπάθεια*), a spacious experience of calm and peace. The passions in this technical formulation are not just about desire—they encompass various problematic states of mind such as depression, hatred and fear. In modern psychological terms, the "passions" are "complexes" or "neuroses"—thickly interwoven tangles of thought, where the different colored threads of emotion and reasoning first need to be teased out. Only then can the resources of consciousness be analyzed, and in their natural state be rewoven, covering the one now "clothed and in [their] right mind" (Mark 5:15).

This dichotomy of view, seeing the passions as either a help or a hindrance, is present even in some of the earliest Christian texts. Those ancient desert psychoanalysts of the soul, such as Isaiah of Scetis (d. 491), saw the energy at the root of the passions as essentially good. In his discourse *On the Natural State of the Intellect*, Isaiah says:

> I do not want you to forget, brothers, that in the beginning, when Adam was created, God placed him in paradise with healthy senses that were established according to nature . . . Desire is the natural state of the intellect because without desire for God there is no love . . . Anger, too, is the natural state of the intellect for without anger we cannot even attain purity unless we are angry toward all that which is sown in us by the enemy.[5]

At source, the passions are an innocent part of the created nature of humanity. The problem is that they have been misdirected away from their original purpose. So, anger as such is not the problem—it is a useful energy to be directed towards purity of heart. Desire as such is not the problem—it is a God-given longing to be directed towards the ultimately desirable goodness of God. Perhaps it would be better to acknowledge this dual aspect of the passions by talking of "afflictive passion" as opposed to "effective passion," to indicate the difference between the two states of mind: the one an unhealthy addiction, the other a flourishing sobriety. It is certainly a theme that emerges again, as we shall see in the writings of Diadochus of Photike (c. 400–486) and Maximus the Confessor (580–662).

For Evagrius, the passions in their negative sense tend to be of more concern, absorbing more of his attention than their corresponding virtues. They are not only unhelpful in the spiritual life, they can lead on to an overwhelming sadness or despair, and a longing for the opportunity to begin again, to start afresh with the slate wiped clean:

> Against the demon that brings to me the sins of my youth: *Everything old has passed away; see, everything has become new (2 Cor. 5.17).*[6]

"Do not remember the sins of my youth or my transgressions," says the psalmist (Ps 25:7), in a passage that Evagrius would have chanted frequently. But he doesn't allow himself to be caught. Here he sees that to be forever remembering the sins of the past is itself a kind of temptation. The soul in ascent to God needs to take wings and fly beyond a fixation on the failings of the past. If we have truly repented our sins, then forever remembering them is a denial of God's forgiveness.

The Eight Thoughts

Evagrius had left the city of Constantinople for the deserts of Egypt to face down the whirling thoughts of his mind, to discover a sense of equilibrium and peace. To this end he formulated a list of "Eight Thoughts" as a way to disarm the mental states that so distressed him. Sometimes he described them as demons, using the language of his age, acknowledging their strength and volatility; sometimes he spoke more dispassionately of "thoughts" (*λογίσμοι/logismoi*), trains of sequential thinking that could leave havoc in their wake. These he itemized as follows:

> There are eight general and basic categories of thoughts in which are included every thought. First is that of gluttony, then impurity, avarice, sadness, anger, *acedia* [sloth, listlessness], vainglory, and last of all, pride. It is not in our power to determine whether we are disturbed by these thoughts, but it is up to us to decide if they are to linger within us or not and whether or not they are to stir up our passions.[7]

This list of thoughts became more widely known in the formulation of Pope Gregory the Great (c. 540–604), reclassified as the "seven deadly sins," with the amalgamation of sadness and sloth, and vainglory and pride, and with the addition of envy. Evagrius seems to have been familiar with them all! Such thoughts are not seen as necessarily sinful, only becoming so when provocation (*προσβολή/prosbole*) is met with assent (*συγκατάθεσις/sunkatathesis*) and allowed to take over the mind as full-blown passion (*πάθος/pathos*). The important thing is to create some distance between the observing mind and the afflictive thoughts, realizing that these are no more than processes of association. They are momentary configurations of the mind, not enduring structures that cannot be changed. Thoughts come and go, and seeing them, and giving them a label, may be the first step in the journey to liberation:

> If there is any monk who wishes to take the measure of some of the more fierce demons so as to gain experience in his monastic art, then let him keep careful watch over his thoughts. Let him observe their intensity, their periods of decline and follow them as they rise and fall. Let him note well the complexity of his thoughts, their periodicity, the demons which cause them, with the order of their succession and the nature of their associations. Then let him ask from Christ the explanations of these data he has observed. For the demons become thoroughly infuriated with those who practice active virtue in a manner that is increasingly contemplative.[8]

This is the beginning of contemplative prayer, a necessary spring clean before the dust is too settled in the recesses of the mind. The person adopting this method of prayer may even find that it seems to make things worse to begin with. But that is not a problem—it is all part of the process. This is the skill of watchfulness (*νηψις/ nepsis*) or attentiveness (*προσοχή/ prosochē*), the guarding of the heart. Realizing just how crowded the mind is becomes the beginning of a stepping back from the crowd, discreetly exiting the dance floor of the nightclub of the mind, and walking out into the cool, refreshing air of a night sky full of stars.

Food for thought

First in the list of thoughts is gluttony (*γαστριμαργία/gastrimargía*), rooted for Evagrius in the memory "that recalls delicacies of the past and remembers pleasant wines and the cups that we used to hold in our hands when we would recline at table and drink."[9]

> Against the thoughts that entice us to be comforted with a little treat of vegetables:
> *The weak eat vegetables (Rom. 14.2).*[10]

> Against the thought that depicts in us severe weakness from diseases that are about to arise in us from fasting, and that persuades us to eat a little cooked food:
> *For whenever I am weak, then I am strong (2 Cor. 12.10).*[11]

Evagrius is plainly conflicted about the issue of food. His desire for "a little treat of vegetables" is quashed by a parental voice demanding abstinence, like a child being denied a solitary ice cream. Probably Evagrius, like so many of the saints through the ages, was too stern on himself, too enamored of the lightness of body and spirit that can accompany a disciplined regime of fasting and prayer. It is likely that he cut short his life by the severity of his eating habits, and particularly his restricted water intake, which may have given him kidney stones.

Evagrius was not above a creative use of Scripture. Notice the exegetical sleight of hand in the passage above: the quote "the weak eat vegetables" was originally written in the context of St. Paul's exhortation to the Christians in Rome to eat meat with a clear conscience. Evagrius has used it to discourage not just eating meat but even to refrain from cooked vegetables. Theologians of his day used more creativity in their exposition of Scripture than most modern critics would allow. Nevertheless, this was standard practice in the ancient world: the meaning of a text was found in its current application, often using ingenious allegorical interpretations, rather than being limited to the original author's supposed intention.

Looking to the interests of others

Continuing the exploration of the afflictive thoughts we read that greed is not only expressed in desire for food; money is also a prime distraction in the religious life. Under the heading of "Concerning Love of Money" (*φιλαργυρία/philarguría*), Evagrius first seems to remember his own past, before seeing the deleterious effect of avarice on his current community life:

> Against the thoughts that remind us of home and property and of the way of life associated with them:
> *'Vanity of vanities,' said the Preacher, 'vanity of vanities: all is vanity! (Eccles. 1.2).*[12]

We may well ask, did he have to remember his home and family so harshly? And yet it was not so much his particular family that he had distanced himself from, but rather the whole interconnected fabric of social norms and expectations surrounding him in the capital of the Byzantine empire. He seems to have recognized that, as with all monastics, it was no use spending his time yearning for a way of life that he had freely chosen to let go. After all, it was his family's comparative wealth and connections that enabled him to rise in society, just as much as his intellectual talents. An education such as he received was only available to the rich. But then perhaps he is just echoing his patron Basil of Caesarea, expensively educated at Athens, but who later scorned (eloquently!) the vanities of academia.

The theme of going into exile (*ξενιτιά/xenitia*) was common in the writings of the desert elders, as we will see in Chapter 2 on the wisdom of Amma Syncletica. It was there, in the poverty of the desert, that true riches were to be found. Simplicity and generosity were essential for opening the locked doors of the heart. For Evagrius the key to the treasury of the heart is kindness:

> Against the thoughts of love of money that corrupt kindness to the brothers:
> *And be kind to one another, tender-hearted, forgiving one another, as God in Christ has forgiven you (Eph. 4.32).*[13]

This is where Evagrius really shines: not in looking back with vague nostalgia and regret, but looking around him at the circle of brothers at his side, all those looking to him for an example of how to live the common life. Avarice holds one's brother or sister as unworthy of our generosity, a sin against kindness and respect. Withholding forgiveness is just as much a sin against God as the stockpiling of worldly goods, and a denial of all that Christ did in his incarnation, becoming poor and so making many rich. Again, Evagrius seeks to hone his vision to see clearly the essentials of life, observing with the writer of the First Letter to Timothy that "we brought nothing into the world, so that we can take nothing out of it; but if we have food and clothing, we will be content with these . . . For the love of money is a root of all kinds of evil" (1 Tim 6:7-10).

In his book *On Thoughts*, Evagrius gives a detailed exposition of how this kind of analysis of thoughts might take place:

> When one of the enemies draws near to wound you and you want 'to turn his sword', as it is written, 'against his own heart' [Ps. 37.15], then do as I tell you. Analyse within yourself the thought that has been sent by him against you: which is it; of how many things is it composed; and which among them chiefly afflicts the mind? What I mean is this. Let us suppose the thought of avarice is sent by him. Analyse this into the mind that received it, the concept of gold, the gold as such, and the avaricious passion; finally, ask which of these is the sin. Is it the mind and, if so, how? For the mind is the icon of God. Is it the concept of gold, then? Who in his right mind would say that? Is the gold as such a sin? Then why was it created? It follows, then, that the cause of the sin is the fourth [avaricious passion], which is neither a thing that subsists in essence, nor a concept of a thing, nor yet a bodiless mind; instead, it is a certain misanthropic pleasure born from self-determination which forces the mind to use God's creations badly and which the law of God has been entrusted to excise. Now as you scrutinise these things, the thought will be dissolved in this contemplation and thus destroyed; the demonic [thought] will flee from you as your thinking is raised on high by this knowledge.[14]

Evagrius is working with the enquiry into what is really the problem in this situation. Is it the mind itself, the money, the thought of money? All these are essentially innocent of offence. The problem is the attachment to the money, the avaricious passion, not the money itself.

A similar dynamic works itself out in many monasteries and convents and other places of silent meditation. Often in prayer we can be distracted by a thousand things—sounds outside the window, gurglings of heating or digestive systems, stray memories that wander into the mind and buzz around like a restless bluebottle. But where is the problem? Is it in the window or the radiator, or your neighbor's active stomach, or the capacity to recall the past? Is it not in the workings of the mind, specifically the irritation that we allow to build up? The problem is not in the pneumatic drill outside your window, but in the mind that (silently) shouts: "Stop that infernal noise!"

Such mental debates may seem complicated, and it would be unhelpful to spend too much time on this preparatory stage of prayer, but it is nonetheless a useful exercise in mindfulness of thinking. This is an exploration of the mind as if it were a jungle full of strange sounds and odors, with shrieks and rustlings that hint of fabulous beasts or tiny, poisonous insects. But in the hand of the explorer there is a reliable map that has been made by those who have already forged the way through. A psychological machete may be needed to cut down the undergrowth, but there is a clear way ahead leading to a cool lake in which to drink and swim. This exploration is a preliminary stage in the journey of prayer, but it is an essential part of the expedition. The beasts discovered do not need to be captured and carried back to a zoo—they just need to be observed and then let go. It is enough to see the thoughts; they return to their natural habitat by their own paths soon enough. The important thing for now is to remain clear-headed and to reach the destination.

Do not let the sun go down on your anger

So far we have looked at the thoughts of attraction, the "appetitive faculty" in the human soul (*τὸ ἐπιθυμητικόν/to epithumetikon*). Evagrius then goes on to explore anger and its companions, the thoughts of the "incensive faculty" (*τὸ θυμικόν/to thumikon*), the aversion, even hatred, hot or frozen, that saps the vitality of life.

Perhaps surprisingly, the next item on Evagrius' list is "Concerning the Thoughts of the Demon of Sadness." It may be that he includes the word "demon" in the title of this chapter as an acknowledgement that sadness (*λύπη/lupe*) is one of the most difficult of thoughts to overcome. It is placed first in the list after the sections on desire for food, sex and money as it represents the failure of desire when left unsatisfied. For Evagrius, sadness is closely linked to grief (the loss of what is desired) and fear (the dread of losing that which is only tenuously held). It is not only about the loss of material things: it is the mind itself that he fears to lose:

> To the Lord concerning the demon that in my intellect threatens me with madness and mental illness, to the shame of me and of those who seek the Lord through the monastic life: *Do not let those who wait on you, Lord of hosts, be ashamed on my account. Do not let those who seek you, God of Israel, be embarrassed because of me (Ps. 69.6).*[15]

This chapter has a strangely modern flavor. Mental illness is increasingly being acknowledged and diagnosed. It comes in many forms and can be exacerbated by social isolation, as was painfully revealed during the Covid pandemic. Many of the monks and nuns in the Egyptian deserts spent long hours alone, and for those whose health was less robust it could have been a cause of mental breakdown. There are, of course, many forms of mental illness. Now that we live so much longer, at least in the developed world, the chances of us being submerged in dementia are increasing by the day. The loss of self-consciousness and memory must be one of the cruelest of fates. "Who are these people who are visiting me? What are they doing in my house?"—these are the distressing questions that bewilder many today. Evagrius faces up to the possible loss of his most prized possession—his own mind—and acknowledges the fear that gnaws at him from within. And yet he does find, as ever, some comfort in the Scriptures, and particularly in the Psalms. Memorized sacred texts can be the last refuge of a fading mind. The disciplines of silence that can help to clarify awareness include the recitation of texts that keep the mind focused and calm. A religious person can sometimes find great comfort in the last days of lucidity by singing, perhaps together with an unknown visitor, the still known and remembered words of a much-loved hymn.

Following on from sadness, Evagrius continues with an analysis of one of the more elemental thoughts: the Demon of Anger (*ὀργή/orgé*).

> Against the intellect that by means of thoughts stirs up conflict in its thinking:
> *The Lord's slave must not be quarrelsome, but kindly to everyone (2 Tim. 2.24).*[16]

Again, it is the importance of kindness that becomes the crux of the matter. "Be angry but do not sin; do not let the sun go down on your anger" (Eph 4:26) says St. Paul to the Ephesians, in a verse often quoted by the desert fathers and mothers of the early church. Acknowledge your own anger, but do not cherish it; do your best to make amends with your estranged brother or sister rather than clinging on to the unhealthy self-righteousness of resentment and hate.

Akedia, *the noonday demon*

Next comes the demon of *akedia* (ἀκηδία), or *accidie* as it is sometimes spelled in its latinized form. Most often it is a term left untranslated, owing to the complexity of this thought. It is compared to sloth or listlessness or sheer boredom, all of which are seen as afflictions particularly affecting those living a solitary life. For the monks and nuns of the Egyptian and Palestinian deserts this was a personal choice, fleeing from the newly burgeoning cities and going out with the express purpose of wrestling with the demons thought to dwell in the wilderness. Today, again as the result of our increasingly atomized existence in the West, this is more likely to be an unchosen vocation, often an unwelcomed experience of loneliness and fear. In Evagrius' day the demon of *akedia* was seen as the archetypal challenge of the hermit life, a state of mind he had clearly seen in others and experienced in himself. His description of the affliction is a classic of the genre, revealing a keen eye and a gently ironic sense of humor, and is worth quoting at some length:

> The demon of acedia, also called the noonday demon (cf. Ps. 90.6), is the most oppressive of all the demons. He attacks the monk about the fourth hour [viz. 10 a.m.] and besieges his soul until the eighth hour [2 p.m.]. First of all, he makes it appear

> that the sun moves slowly or not at all, and that the day seems to be fifty hours long. Then he compels the monk to look constantly towards the windows, to jump out of the cell, to watch the sun to see how far it is from the ninth hour [3 p.m.], to look this way and that lest one of the brothers . . . and further, he instils in him a dislike for the place and for his state of life itself, for manual labour, and also the idea that love has disappeared from among the brothers and there is no one to console him. And should there be someone during those days who has offended the monk, this too the demon uses to add further to his dislike of the place.[17]

The hapless monk stands staring out of the window, hoping that someone might happen to call by in need of the attention of hospitality, thus giving him an excuse for avoiding his dilatory prayers. The ninth hour would be eagerly awaited as this was the time of the only meal of the day, one of the few (rather paltry) opportunities for sensory pleasure. Even the language of the text echoes the listlessness of the solitary monk, with sentences trailing off into silence, as seen in the translation quoted above. A myriad of perfectly reasonable proposals for meaningful ministry suggest themselves, all of them at some distance from the monk's cell, and all of which he is sure are his Christian duty to fulfil. Meanwhile, the failure of the communal life where he lives is blamed squarely on others, never on the afflicted monk himself. Should he try to set himself to study rather than pray, the result is even more comic:

> When he reads, the one afflicted with acedia yawns a lot and readily drifts off into sleep; he rubs his eyes and stretches his arms; turning his eyes away from the book, he stares at the wall and again goes back to reading for a while; leafing through the pages, he looks curiously for the end of texts, he counts the folios and calculates the number of gatherings. Later, he closes the book and puts it under his head and falls asleep, but not a very deep sleep, for hunger then rouses his soul and has him show concern for its needs.[18]

It is a scene re-enacted in every university and monastic library across the world. How entertaining is a simple mathematical equation compared to analyzing the Trinity, or simply learning how to watch the breath come and go? 'If I read a page every two minutes, a chapter in half an hour, then I'll be finished by tea time. Shall I have a biscuit also or just a little bit of toast . . . ?'

The demon of pride

Having explored the outer reaches of the mind's solar system, Evagrius finishes with two interrelated thoughts: vainglory (*κενοδοξία*/*kenodoxía*) and pride (*ὑπερηφανία*/*huperephanía*). Later lists amalgamated the two, but there is a subtle difference to notice between them. Vainglory is a kind of preening of the self at one's uncommon prowess, one's skill and ability that distinguishes self from others. Pride is more visceral, more fundamental: a proclamation of one's stature based not on what I have done, but simply as a result of who I am. Of course there is a good type of pride also. In the Christian tradition it can be an acknowledgement of one's creation in the image of God. In this sense all is grace: I am an inalienable part of the body of Christ, cherished with an undying love by the Creator who fashioned me and breathed life into me.

In the list of the thoughts, matters are not so noble:

> Against the thought of vainglory that advises me sternly to withdraw from the brotherhood and to cloister myself from the brothers, supposing that they lead me astray:
> *The proud have hidden a snare for me (Ps. 140.5).*[19]

If only I could find the perfect church/monastery/partner/job/ house, then everything would be so much easier! It can be so pleasurable, in a rather glutinous way, to itemize the ways others hold us back. Maybe it is us being a stumbling block to them! Vainglory is rather simple to diagnose, compared to the intricacies of pride:

> Against the thought of pride that glorifies me on the pretext that I edify souls with a stable way of life and knowledge of God:
> *Unless the Lord builds the house, the builders labour in vain; unless the Lord guards the city, guards keep watch in vain (Ps. 127.1).*[20]

Clearly Evagrius struggled with pride, but he is aware of the struggle, and that is the most important thing. Should he give up trying to edify others on the grounds that he is good at it and knows that he is? There is a kind of reverse pride, after all, that refuses to act on the grounds of humility. But is it really humility to deny that God's grace has done anything for me, and for others through me, if I let it be so? Just one step out of the limelight is enough for God to work with, and God is not too proud to be God. But enough of these subtle distinctions. Pride can be rather more direct:

> Against the demon that said to me, 'Look, you have become a perfect monk':
> *There is hope because a living dog is better than a dead lion (Eccles. 9.4).*[21]

"I may be a mongrel of a monk," says Evagrius, "but at least I am alive. Where there is breath there is hope." And dogs are useful too. Evagrius says elsewhere: "The mind engaged in contemplation is like a dog, for through the movement of the irascible part it chases away all impassioned thoughts."[22] Perhaps better than either a dog or a lion: to be one who rejoices in all that is good.

The true theologian

We have been looking at one particular formulation that classifies the practical aspects of prayer: the list of the Eight Thoughts. Now it is time to look in more depth at the overall structure of the Christian life as described by Evagrius. He often uses the literary form of 100 "chapters," that is, 100 (or thereabouts) short paragraphs of gnomic wisdom; he may even have been the inventor of this literary form. The first three "chapters" of Evagrius' work *Praktikos* sum up the span of his teaching and, incidentally, that of the early church theologians Clement of Alexandria (c. 150–c. 215) and Origen (c. 185–c. 253):

1. Christianity is the dogma of Christ our Savior. It is composed of *praktike* [*πρακτική*, the practical, ascetic life], of the contemplation of the physical world and of the contemplation of God.
2. The Kingdom of Heaven is *apatheia* (*ἀπάθεια*) of the soul along with true knowledge of existing things.
3. The Kingdom of God is knowledge (*γνῶσις/gnosis*) of the Holy Trinity co-extensive with the capacity of the intelligence and giving it a surpassing incorruptibility.[23]

First there is *praktike*—the ascetic life of fasting, prayer and vigils, including the struggle with the Eight Thoughts and their derivatives. This clarifies and calms the mind and leads, second, to "true knowledge of existing things," that is, contemplation of God through the creation (*θεωρία φυσική/theoria physike*). This is the "Kingdom of Heaven," or of Christ, and refers to the knowledge of nature, and of the beings that comprise the natural world. Finally, the "Kingdom of God" is theology proper, that is, the knowledge and contemplation of God in God's self (*γνῶσις θεοῦ/gnosis theou*), in the pristine clarity of the ineffable Godhead.

In his work *To Monks in Monasteries and Communities*, Evagrius gives a Eucharistic flavor to these three stages:

> Flesh of Christ, the practical virtues; one who eats of it shall become impassible.
> Blood of Christ, contemplation of beings; one who drinks it will receive wisdom from him.
> Breast of the Lord, knowledge of God; one who reclines on it will be endowed with theology.[24]

This formulation brings out the fact that liturgy was an essential part of the path described by Evagrius. He sometimes comes across as a religious psychoanalyst, probing the thoughts and fantasies of his clients. But, primarily, Evagrius was a monk, whose life centered on daily prayer and the liturgies celebrated together with his brothers when they gathered each weekend. He was a deacon not a priest, but that was so that he could maintain his desert seclusion and not be packed off to a city or be overwhelmed by pastoral duties in a busy urban parish. There are several stories of desert fathers doing all they can to avoid bishops who might ordain them against their will.

The first of the three stages of the path as outlined above is the spiritual discipline that leads to an awareness of the passions, and their root in the cherishing of the self at the expense of others. The second stage is described as "natural contemplation" (*θεωρία φυσική/theoria physike*). This is an invitation to contemplate the "spiritual essences" of things, their *logoi* (*λόγοι*). Julia Konstantinovsky says of this stage:

> Just as in the Eucharist the physical bread and wine are sacramentally changed, so in natural contemplation the mind's eye perceives the materiality of the universe become transfigured by grace. The universe is then revealed as the locus, at once physical and spiritual, of God's graceful self-revelation. Through contemplation, the seeing mind interiorizes the cosmic drama, thus, from an observer, becoming a participant and finally the locus par excellence of God's encounter with the universe. In this way the mind is transformed into the 'true church' of God, where the cosmic liturgy takes place. In this encounter, both the corporeality and immateriality of the universe and of man are inseparably intertwined. The idea of matter that emerges from this conception of natural contemplation is overwhelmingly positive. Matter is hallowed; it is spiritual; it is transformational. Like the Eucharist and the Scripture, the material universe is sacramental.[25]

Such an understanding of natural contemplation dispels the idea that Evagrius is wedded to a Platonic dualism that downgrades the body as a mere hindrance to the immortal aethereal soul. For all his emphasis on the importance of ascesis, spiritual struggle with the physical senses and desires, still the body itself is like a crystal, letting the light of eternity shine through it at every sparkling turn.

Intrinsic in this whole process is the importance of love. Theology, here the climax of the path, is the experience of the Beloved Disciple who leaned against the heart of Jesus at the Last Supper, and who has become known as St. John the Theologian (cf. John 13:25; 21:20). The model of the ideal disciple is the one who loved and was beloved. Integral to the journey to union with God is the experience of love. The purpose of developing a calm mind is simply to enable one to see more clearly and so to love with all one's heart and without distraction:

> The state of prayer can be aptly described as a habitual state of imperturbable calm (*apatheia*). It snatches to the heights of intelligible reality the spirit which loves wisdom and which is truly spiritualized by the most intense love (*ἀγάπη/agape*).[26]

Theology, the vision of God, is for Evagrius a kind of prayer. One of his most famous sayings was: "If you are a theologian you truly pray. If you truly pray you are a theologian."[27] For him the place to discover the love and knowledge of God was not the lecture halls of Athens or the library of Alexandria but the caves of the desert, and more particularly, the cave of the heart. There he could find true knowledge and know what it was to be a theologian lost in love.

The sapphire light of the mind

It is at this point that the path mapped out by Evagrius takes a different turn: here he moves from making full use of concepts and language, known as a kataphatic approach to God, and seeks rather to go beyond language, in an apophatic way, beyond all descriptions of God. He says in *Reflections*:

> If someone should want to behold the state of his mind, let him deprive himself of all mental representations, and then he shall behold himself resembling sapphire or the colour of heaven. It is impossible to accomplish this without impassibility, for he will need God to collaborate with him and breathe into him the connatural light.[28]

The reference here seems to be to Exodus 24:9-10, where Moses and Aaron and 70 of the elders of Israel ascend Mount Sinai: "And they saw the God of Israel. Under his feet there was something like a pavement of sapphire stone, like the very heaven for clearness." This sky-blue light which irradiates the place where God dwells is seen not just in heaven but in the mind and heart of men and women, God's dwelling place and home. This is the new self spoken of by St. Paul writing to the Colossians: "you have stripped off the old self with its practices and have clothed yourselves with the new self, which is being renewed in knowledge according to the image of its creator" (Col 3:9-10). This luminosity of spirit only shines out when all worldly desires have been renounced and all mental representations of God have been relinquished. Then it can be known that "prayer is a state of the mind that arises under the influence of the unique light of the Holy Trinity."[29]

Evagrius was uncertain at first what this meant, though he clearly experienced it himself. In the end he and a monastic friend went to another elder to receive guidance on whether or not to trust this vision of light:

> Concerning this light, I and God's servant Ammonias wanted to know where it comes from, and we asked the holy John, the seer of Thebes, whether it is the nature of the intellect to be luminous and thus it pours forth the light from itself or whether it [the light] appears from something else outside and illumines it [the intellect]; but he answered and said, 'No human being is able to explain this, and indeed, apart from the grace of God the intellect cannot be illumined in prayer by being set free from the many cruel enemies that are endeavouring to destroy it.'[30]

In the end, John of Thebes rather dodges the question, encouraging his questioners not to give up their ascetic struggles, but his basic answer is that illumination in prayer can only come by the grace of God, and so Evagrius and his friend are encouraged to speak about this and experience it further. He writes that it is the fruit of *apatheia*, love and wisdom, for after the diligent practice of moderation, vigilance and virtue, "then imperturbability of heart will arise for you and in prayer you will see your mind like a star."[31]

The beatitude of prayer

Finally let us return to Evagrius' treatise *On Prayer* for some practical words of encouragement:

> Happy is the monk who views the welfare and progress of all with as much joy as if it were his own.
> Happy is the monk who considers all people as god—after God.
> A monk is a man who is separated from all and who is in harmony with all.
> A monk is a man who considers himself one with all people because he seems constantly to see himself in everyone.[32]

"The monk" is anyone who sincerely practices the spiritual disciplines and, by the grace of God, is led to the experience of contemplating God in creation, and in the stillness of the human mind lost in love. In this state the barriers between self and other begin to break down. There is no progress in prayer that excludes others. Withdrawal to the desert (or the monastery, or the city for that matter) is only a stage in the realization that all are united in the one body of Christ. Happy and blessed are the men and women who know this for themselves, who see God at the still center of all things. What more is to be said?

> At a meeting of the hermits in Cellia, Evagrius made a speech. Then the priest there said, 'Evagrius, we know that if you were in your own country, perhaps you would already be a bishop, ruling over many. Here you are only a pilgrim.' Evagrius was pierced to the heart at these words, but he bent his head calmly and without haste and looked at the ground, then wrote in the dust with his finger, and said, 'Truly, brothers, that is right. But, as it is written, "I have spoken once and I will no more answer"' (Job 40.5).[33]

And having said that he went back to his prayers.

Questions for reflection and discussion

- Do you find the classification of the "Eight Thoughts" helpful?
- Which of the thoughts is the most difficult to overcome? Why?
- Is "dispassion" a necessary quality in prayer and in everyday life?

Further reading

Robert E. Sinkewicz (trans.), 2003, *Evagrius of Pontus: The Greek Ascetic Corpus*, Oxford: Oxford University Press.

William Harmless SJ, 2004, *Desert Christians: An Introduction to the Literature of Early Monasticism*, Oxford: Oxford University Press. \

Gabriel Bunge, 2002, *Earthen Vessels: The Practice of Personal Prayer According to the Patristic Tradition*, San Francisco, CA: Ignatius Press.

Notes

1 Robert T. Meyer, 1964, *Palladius: The Lausiac History*, Ancient Christian Writers, New York: Paulist Press, p. 110.

2 William Harmless SJ, 2004, *Desert Christians: An Introduction to the Literature of Early Monasticism*, Oxford: Oxford University Press, p. 363.

3 *Antirrhetikos* 2.35; David Brakke, 2009, *Evagrius of Pontus: Talking Back (Antirrhetikos), a Monastic Handbook for Combating Demons*, Collegeville, MN: Cistercian Publications, p. 77.

4 *Praktikos* 4; John Eudes Bamberger OCSO, 1981, *Evagrius Ponticus: The Praktikos & Chapters on Prayer*, Collegeville, MN: Cistercian Publications, p. 16.

5 John Cryssavgis (trans.) with Pachomios Penkett, 2002, *Abba Isaiah of Scetis: Ascetic Discourses*, Collegeville, MN: Cistercian Publications, pp. 43–5.

6 *Antirrhetikos* 4.73; Brakke, *Talking Back*, p. 116.

7 *Praktikos* 6; Bamberger, *Evagrius Ponticus*, pp. 16–17.

8 *Praktikos* 50; Bamberger, *Evagrius Ponticus*, pp. 29–30.

9 *Antirrhetikos* 1.30; Brakke, *Talking Back*, p. 59.

10 *Antirrhetikos* 1.53; Brakke, *Talking Back*, p. 64.

11 *Antirrhetikos* 1.59; Brakke, *Talking Back*, p. 65.

12 *Antirrhetikos* 3.34; Brakke, *Talking Back*, p. 92.

13 *Antirrhetikos* 3.48; Brakke, *Talking Back*, p. 95.

14 *Thoughts* 19; A. M. Casiday, 2006, *Evagrius Ponticus*, London: Routledge, p. 102.

15 *Antirrhetikos* 4.43; Brakke, *Talking Back*, p. 109.

16 *Antirrhetikos* 5.55; Brakke, *Talking Back*, p. 130.

17 *Praktikos* 12; Robert E. Sinkewicz (trans.), 2003, trans. *Evagrius of Pontus: The Greek Ascetic Corpus*, Oxford: Oxford University Press, p. 99.

18 *Eight Thoughts* 15; Sinkewicz, *The Greek Ascetic Corpus*, p. 84.

19 *Antirrhetikos* 7.11; Brakke, *Talking Back*, p. 149.

20 *Antirrhetikos* 8.30; Brakke, *Talking Back*, p. 166.

21 *Antirrhetikos* 8.39; Brakke, *Talking Back*, p. 167.

22 *Reflections* 9; Sinkewicz, *The Greek Ascetic Corpus*, p. 211.

23 *Praktikos* 1–3, Bamberger, *Evagrius Ponticus*, pp. 15–16.

24 *To Monks* 118–120; Sinkewicz, *The Greek Ascetic Corpus*, p. 130.

25 Julia Konstantinovsky, 2016, *Evagrius Ponticus: The Making of a Gnostic*, London: Routledge, p. 47.

26 *Prayer* 52; Bamberger, *Evagrius Ponticus*, p. 63.

27 *Prayer* 60; Bamberger, *Evagrius Ponticus*, p. 65.

28 *Reflections* 2; Sinkewicz, *The Greek Ascetic Corpus*, p. 211.

29 *Reflections* 27; Sinkewicz, *The Greek Ascetic Corpus*, p. 213.

30 *Antirrhetikos* 6.16; Brakke, *Talking Back*, p. 137.

31 *Thoughts* 43; Casiday, *Evagrius Ponticus*, p. 116.

32 *Prayer* 122–5; Bamberger, *Evagrius Ponticus*, pp. 75–6.

33 Benedicta Ward SLG, 2003, *The Desert Fathers: Sayings of the Early Christian Monks*, London: Penguin Books, p. 172.

2

Syncletica of Alexandria and the Desert Mothers

The flight into the deserts of Egypt and Palestine in the fourth century of the Common Era was one of the most distinctive aspects of the early Christian church. In the literature depicting this movement, and the sayings of those who made the journey to these remote monasteries and hermitages, there was plenty of material to inspire the Christians newly liberated from state oppression. This was a new kind of martyrdom: no longer were Christians thrown to the lions in the Roman amphitheaters or burnt at the stake rather than abjure their faith. A new challenge was needed, and the deserts provided for some an arena for heroic witness to the faith. For others the monastic life may have seemed a natural path to follow, after the example of Jewish celibate communities such as the Essenes at Qumran or the Therapeutae at Alexandria, or even due to possible contact with Buddhist monastics at Roman port cities or on the silk road to China. The Christian New Testament itself contains sufficient warrant for this kind of life in community, with its depiction of the apostles living together having all things in common (Acts 2:44-47), and St Paul encouraging a celibate life in devotion to Christ (1 Cor 7:8). Just hearing the gospel message of Jesus of Nazareth to leave home and family and to follow him was enough for some, like Antony the Great, to sell all they possessed, give the money to the poor, and to seek God in solitude or in the company of like-minded women or men.

Various other reasons may have influenced the flight to the desert monasteries. There may have been economic factors, with some fleeing the cities and towns to avoid the burden of unpayable taxes. Or it may have been a prevailing sense of anxiety at the time, with rumors of wars and earthquakes, and an expectation of the imminent end of all things. For some it was an opportunity to escape punishment for crimes, or to repent of such criminal activity, or even to avoid conscription into the army. The exact motivation is often unclear and a number of factors may have influenced individual decisions.

But who was making this intrepid journey from home and family to the caves and hermitages of these new "cities of the desert"? Browsing through the literature of the sayings of the wise monastics you could get the impression that only men were able to do this, and only a handful of women were able to make the same leap from family ties. In fact we don't know how many female hermits and other monastics made this choice, but there were certainly more than just a few. Rufinus, in his "History of the Monks of Egypt," recording a pilgrimage made in the year 394, doesn't mention a single female ascetic of any renown. Palladius, however, in his *Lausiac History* written in the year 420, devotes several chapters to the women he encountered on his monastic travels, and is plainly inspired by their lives. He talks of women such as Alexandra who left the city of Alexandria and went to live, like the proto-typical hermit Antony the Great, in seclusion in a tomb. Food and water were handed to her through a window, and for ten years she looked no one in the face. When asked what she did to survive such a strict enclosure she replied:

> 'From early dawn to the ninth hour [3 p.m.] I pray from hour to hour while spinning flax. The rest of the time I go over in my mind the [stories and writings of the] holy patriarchs, prophets, apostles, and martyrs. Then I eat my crusts and wait patiently the other hours for my end with good hope.'[1]

It would be good to know how she prayed, both while spinning and while resting after her meal. Probably she repeated a single line from the Psalms, or recited the whole Psalter as a way of memorizing and internalizing the text. At any rate, she persevered for ten years in this ascetic regimen before "falling asleep" and being discovered by those who finally broke through the door. Another holy woman, by the name of Piamoun, who spent her time spinning flax with her mother and eating only every other day, was renowned for her gift of prophecy. When two villages came to blows over the distribution of river water it was Piamoun the villagers turned to as mediator in the conflict. She had already been warned about the conflict by the message of an angel, and duly achieved reconciliation by her prayers, which miraculously glued the warring parties to the spot so that they couldn't move or exchange blows.

Besides holy hermits, religious women also gathered in great numbers in monasteries organized by Pachomius (c. 292–348), one of the founders of Christian coenobitic communities. Palladius describes the monastery Pachomius founded for men at Tabennisi on the River Nile, numbering more than 1,000 monks, all with trades and tasks such as tailors, metalworkers, carpenters, gardeners and those responsible for the camels and pigs. He goes on to say:

> In addition to these there was also a monastery of some four hundred women. They had the same sort of management and the same way of life, except for their clothing. The women lived on one side of the river opposite the men. When a virgin died, the others laid her out for burial, and they carried her body and placed it on the bank of the river. The brethren would cross on a ferry-boat and carrying palm leaves and olive branches bring the body over and bury it in the common cemetery.[2]

Thus, in life and death the men and women in community supported each other and devoted themselves to prayer and good works. The sexes may not have lived directly alongside each other, but the manner of life and the goal of their practice was parallel and mutually beneficial. A life of communal obedience freed the monastic to be able to search within their heart and to overcome by grace the *logismoi*, the afflictive patterns of thought so clearly elucidated by Evagrius. Rousseau summarizes the ascetic goal of the Pachomian monasteries:

> Fear, even of demons, could lead to self-awareness. Self-awareness led to self-knowledge and self-discipline. Those when combined brought purity of heart. Purity of heart could make possible the

> vision of God, yes; but also—and for Pachomius, perhaps even more so—it encouraged a keener understanding of one's fellows. Just as freedom came with commitment to a new society, so self-possession in the presence of God was shared with others. It was to a great extent defined by that very sharing. Is that a tentative way of suggesting that the final goal for Pachomius, reached by way of vision, was love? Love is a notion that proves elusive in the Pachomian corpus. Fear, purity, knowledge, freedom, goodness, gentleness—all of them are present, but love is less frequently made explicit. 'This is the love of God,' said Pachomius, 'to have compassion for each other.'[3]

Pachomius was not particularly interested in ecstatic visions. Just to see the invisible God made visible in the purity and humility of a human being was quite sufficient. But the complete clarity of such a vision was only possible to those endowed with the gift of discernment, those able to read the thoughts of the heart.

Scholars of the Kingdom of God

As it has already been noted, even a cursory look at the collections of sayings of the desert elders reveals a frustrating absence: there are only a handful of sayings and stories preserved that represent the desert mothers rather than the desert fathers. Consequently, the net has to be cast wider in order to get a picture of the contribution of women to this important movement in the development of the early church. This can be done in part by seeing how the scholarship of women made a major contribution to the self-understanding of the emerging desert movement. One of the longer chapters in the *Lausiac History* is devoted to Melania the Elder, who played such an important part in the life of Evagrius. She was Spanish by birth and became a Roman citizen. She was the daughter of the consul Marcellinus, and the wife of a high-ranking official. Widowed at 22, she set off for Alexandria at full speed in order to maintain her independence. After spending six months in the region, she sold most of her estates and established a monastery in Jerusalem, where she lived for 27 years together with 50 holy nuns. There she became friends with the Italian monk and priest Rufinus, who had also founded a monastery, and the two of them frequently hosted bishops, monks and nuns passing through Jerusalem, supporting them and offering them advice. Finally, after a lifetime of generous donations she sold everything which remained, distributed her wealth, and within 40 days passed away in peace.

Melania was a great scholar, Palladius saying of her:

> She was most erudite and fond of literature, and she turned night into day going through every writing of the ancient commentators—three million lines of Origen and two and a half million lines of Gregory, Stephen, Pierius, Basil, and other worthy men. And she did not read them once only and in an offhand way, but she worked on them, dredging through each work seven or eight times.[4]

Like Paula the Elder (347–404), and the other female scholars gathered around Jerome (c. 342–420), there were in the church many examples of women engaging in study of the Scriptures and becoming highly respected teachers of the faith. A rich Roman widow with time on her hands, Paula embarked on a tour of Egypt and the Holy Land, finally settling in Bethlehem where she founded monasteries both for women and for men, from all social classes. She was a great linguist, learning Hebrew so well that she could chant the Psalms in their original language without an accent. With her linguistic skills and her attention to detail, she collaborated extensively with Jerome in his work producing the Vulgate, the Latin translation of the Bible in a language ordinary people could understand. Paula's determination to give away her wealth and so to follow the example of the poverty of Jesus of Nazareth led to her dying with many debts to pass on to her daughter Eustochium.

Another female theologian was Macrina the Younger (327–379), elder sister of Gregory of Nyssa (c. 335–395), whom Gregory regarded as his own teacher and the one who had brought him to faith by her example and her words. He was devasted when she died, and wrote at length about their last conversation concerning the soul's final journey to God. Macrina had turned their family estate at Annisa in Cappadocia into a monastery for women and men, with each on either side of a river. Simplicity of life, devotion to prayer and recitation of the Scriptures, social equality and care for the sick regardless of status were the principles by which she lived. These became the foundation of the Rules for monastics later written down by another of her brothers, Basil, Bishop of Caesarea.

Palladius also recounts the story of Juliana, another scholar of the faith:

> She took in Origen the writer when he fled from the insurrection of the pagans, and she kept him at her own expense for two years and looked after him . . . In passing I have put in [this book] the virtues of these women so that we may learn that we can gain in many ways if we would.[5]

Palladius says that he found a very old book which had been in the possession of Juliana, and had comments written on it in Origen's own handwriting, testifying to its antiquity going back to about 200 CE. A rare book indeed, now most likely lost forever, or languishing in a dim basement corner of the Bodleian Library in Oxford, waiting for an eager PhD student to blow off the dust and, trembling perhaps, lift open the crisp desiccated cover!

The wisdom of spiritual motherhood

One of the Desert Mothers committed to a life of prayer and study, Amma Theodora, acknowledges the difficulties awaiting anyone who follows this path:

> Amma Theodora said, 'Let us strive to enter by the narrow gate. Just as the trees, if they have not stood before the winter's storms cannot bear fruit, so it is with us; this present age is a storm and it is only through many trials and temptations that we can obtain an inheritance in the kingdom of heaven.'[6]

Cultivating the rule of God in one's heart needs the persistence of a bramble and the patience of an oak. These trials may be as much physical as mental, leading to a kind of lethargy and debility, a kind of long Covid of the soul:

> It is good to live in peace, for the wise person practices perpetual prayer. It is truly a great thing for an ascetic to live in peace, especially for the younger ones. However, you should realize that as soon as you intend to live in peace, at once evil comes and weighs down your soul through *accidie* [sloth], faintheartedness, and evil thoughts. It also attacks your body through sickness, debility, weakening of the knees, and all the members. It dissipates the strength of soul and body, so that one believes one is ill and no longer able to pray. But if we are vigilant, all these temptations fall away.[7]

Sometimes the hardest thing in prayer is not so much the wrestling with an unquiet mind but the battle to stay awake. Here we are in good company, with Peter, James and John in the Garden of Gethsemane, who fail to pray with Jesus as he wrestles with the imminence of the Passion approaching him (Matt 26:40-41). Vigils—long nights spent in lonely prayer—were the stock in trade of the desert monastics. Just to keep awake they would sometimes walk back and forth in their simple dwellings, perhaps also carrying a sack on their shoulders for good measure. Following the exhortation of the psalmist (119:62), "At midnight I rise to praise you, because of your righteous ordinances," they would battle with sleep until the first light of dawn and then begin once again the daily round of prayer.

Theodora goes on to outline the practice of a true teacher of the faith, revealing the principles by which she herself taught others:

> A teacher ought to be a stranger to the desire for domination, vainglory and pride. A teacher should not be fooled by flattery, nor be blinded by gifts, conquered by the stomach, nor dominated by anger. A teacher should be patient, gentle and humble as far as possible; successfully tested and without partisanship, full of concern, and a lover of souls.[8]

As Evagrius recounted in the previous chapter, teaching others is a great temptation to pride, but it also sets up the one who teaches for a fall. In communities of every shape and form, whether religious or secular, there are always some ready to subtly undermine the authority of those in a position of leadership. Flattery and patronage seek to exercise control; even the gift of a baked cake can be a way to compromise the integrity of others; and every attendee of a Parochial Church Council knows the simmering anger of those who claim to know exactly how things have always been done at their particular church. But the true teacher sails a straight course, whether running with the wind or tacking furiously to keep in more-or-less the right direction.

Finally, Theodora offers some wise advice concerning humility as the safest haven for the true ascetic:

> Neither asceticism, nor vigils nor any kind of suffering are able to save, only true humility can do that. There was an anchorite [a solitary hermit] who was able to banish demons; and asked them, 'What makes you go away? Is it fasting?' They replied, 'We do not eat or drink.' 'Is it vigils?' They replied, 'We do not sleep.' 'Is it separation from the world?' 'We live in deserts.' 'What power sends you away then?' They said, 'Nothing can overcome us, but only humility.' 'Do you see how humility is victorious over the demons?'[9]

The tools of the ascetics' trade—fasting, prayer, watchfulness through the silent hours of the night—are of no use without the fundamental virtue of humility. Learn this skill, and the rest will come soon enough.

Mother Syncletica of Alexandria

Of all the women who enriched the life of the church in this period by their humble erudition and heartfelt prayers, Amma Syncletica (380–c. 460) has left the most extensive collection of sayings and stories to encourage the faithful. Syncletica was a beautiful young woman with many suitors attracted by her looks, as well as her family's wealth and high social rank. Urged on by her parents to accept one of these offers, she sought to be betrothed to her heavenly bridegroom, Jesus Christ. She fasted, but not to excess, and managed to keep her devotion to the Lord largely a secret affair. After the death of her parents, she sold the property left to her, gave the proceeds to the poor, and settled together with her blind sister in a family tomb at some distance from the city of Alexandria. There she increased her physical austerities, eating and drinking little, and sleeping for short periods on the ground. Although she preferred to keep silence, yet at the request of the other women gathering around her, she shared the wisdom she had gleaned from the Scriptures and her prayers.

Her teaching often made use of pithy sayings and vibrant images that would stay in the mind. About the difficulties experienced in prayer she said:

> In the beginning there are a great many battles and a good deal of suffering for those who are advancing towards God, and afterwards, ineffable joy. It is like those who wish to light a fire; at first they are choked by the smoke and cry, and by this means obtain what they seek (as it is said: 'Our God is a consuming fire' [Heb. 12.29]): so we also must kindle the divine fire in ourselves through tears and hard work.[10]

The gift of tears and the accompanying compunction are a constant theme in the sayings of the desert monastics. Arsenius was particularly famous for his tears, shedding so many that his eyelashes fell out, and a groove was made in his chest where the tears flowed down. Tears, it was believed, washed the soul clean, the only washing necessary after the cleansing waters of baptism. Tears are described as coming from the heart, which is understood in this tradition not as the root of our emotions, but as the center of our being and where we become united with God. Therefore, the tears are spiritual, not just emotional. Tears unite those who pray in this way to the one of whom the Gospel of John declared, in the shortest verse of the Bible: "Jesus wept" (John 11:35). Just as Jesus also wept over the sins of Jerusalem (Luke 19:41), so the monastics of the desert wept over their own sins and the sins of the cities they had left behind. This was the outer expression of the inward confession of sin, the repentance that leads to life.

Like Evagrius in his depiction of the restlessness of *akedia*, Syncletica advocated a steadfastness of purpose lived out in the stability of staying in one place:

> If you find yourself in a monastery do not go to another place, for that will harm you a great deal. Just as the bird who abandons the eggs she was sitting on prevents them from hatching, so the monk or the nun grows cold and their faith dies, when they go from one place to another.[11]

Here, like Jesus weeping over Jerusalem, Syncletica uses feminine imagery to draw the picture of the monastic as one who broods over her eggs, keeping them warm to ensure that they hatch. Again, the "divine fire" must be kindled and fed, and faith be kept burning in the hearth of the heart, lest by negligence the flames be allowed to burn out and the desire for salvation grow cold.

This use of feminine imagery, and awareness of the trials of women in the ancient world, is a characteristic of Syncletica:

> Let us women not be misled by the thought that those in the world are without cares. For perhaps in comparison they struggle more than we do. For towards women generally there is great hostility in the world. They bear children with difficulty and risk, and they suffer patiently through nursing, and they share illnesses with their sick children—and these things they endure without having any limit to their travail. For either the children they bear are maimed in body, or, brought up in perversity, they treacherously murder their parents. Since we women know these facts, therefore, let us not be deluded by the Enemy that their life is easy and carefree. For in giving birth women die in labour; and yet, in failing to give birth, they waste away under reproaches that they are barren and unfruitful.[12]

Throughout history women have faced great dangers in childbirth and caring for young children. The infant mortality rate under the Roman empire must have been terrifying, perhaps increasing the numbers of those willing to embrace the hardships of monastic life. And yet they can't win—either they die giving birth, or are reproached for failing to give birth and not maintaining the family line. In those days, even if the woman safely produced a child, it was quite likely to be killed by exposure if the husband didn't want to keep it, particularly if the child was a girl. It is not surprising that many young women sought to escape unwanted arranged marriages, perhaps by flight to the desert, or by making the ultimate sacrifice of accepting martyrdom rather than obedience to social norms.

At other times Syncletica uses imagery from the seas and the perils of travel by boat:

> Like a ship our soul is sometimes engulfed by the waves without and is sometimes swamped by the bilge-water within. Certainly we too sometimes perish through sins committed externally, but we sometimes are destroyed by thoughts within us. And so we must guard against onslaughts of spirits from outside us, and bail out impurities of thoughts inside us; and we must always be vigilant with regard to our thoughts, for they are a constant threat to us. Against the storm waves outside salvation often comes from ships nearby when the sailors cry out for help; but bilge-waters overflow and frequently kill the seamen, often when they are asleep and the sea is calm.[13]

Here the thoughts are attacking from all sides—from outside the ship of the soul in the form of waves, and from within by the bilge water seeping through the hull. Like sailors in a midnight storm on the Mediterranean Sea, an experience known well by the intrepid traveler Paul of Tarsus, every possible leak had to be found and filled, and every unnecessary weight thrown overboard. It is the unseen leaks that are the most dangerous and can sink a boat while in a calm sea. So, the boat of the mind must be ceaselessly inspected and repaired, at times removing the boat from the sea altogether, like a long retreat far from the waves, where pitch can be applied wherever there is damage to be found. Maybe Syncletica herself had wandered along the docks of Alexandria, thinking of distant lands, including her own ancestral home of Macedonia, and dreamed of a journey far away.

Elsewhere Syncletica uses the image of a house being demolished from all sides:

> Consequently, the mind must become painstakingly diligent with respect to its thoughts. For when the Enemy wants to destroy the soul as he would a building, he engineers its collapse from the foundations, or he begins from the roof and topples the whole structure; or, he goes in through the windows, ties up the master of the house first and thus wins control of everything. 'Foundation', then, signifies good works, 'roof', 'faith', and 'windows' the senses. And through all of them the Enemy wages war. And so the person wishing to be saved must be very watchful.[14]

Here the imagery is deliberately thought through, not just added for extra color to the tale. It becomes an allegory more than just a parable, a teaching tool for the monastics around her who feel equally besieged on all sides, by the thoughts within and the demons without, no less than the whole of society making impossible demands. Here the devil is portrayed as a kind of crazed operator of a JCB bulldozer, or swinging a wrecking ball as it whistles through the air, crashing into the crumbling masonry of the soul.

In all this Syncletica is showing herself to be a practitioner of the analysis of the soul as systematized by Evagrius Ponticus. In one section she clearly seems to be referring to this way of discerning the thoughts and decoding the secret patterns of the mind:

> I know a servant of God living according to virtue who, while sitting in his cell, observed the occurrences of evil thoughts and kept track of which came first and which second, and of how long a time each one of them persisted, and of whether it occurred later or earlier than on the preceding day. Thus he came to know accurately the grace of God and his own strength and power, and eventually, to be sure, he came to know also the overthrow of the Enemy.[15]

Like so many others, Syncletica was indebted to the sagacity and intellectual astuteness of monastics such as Evagrius. It was only much later that his writings became condemned by some theologians of the early church. At first sight it would seem that this passage is describing Syncletica as indeed a disciple of Evagrius, but she may be obliquely referring to herself. The phrase "I know a servant of God . . ." was sometimes used by monastics out of humility to disguise their own experience. Perhaps this teaching of "*praktike*," practical guidance on the sequences of thought, was a common tradition through which many found a protection in their struggles with the demonic demolition experts of hell.

If they did manage some small triumph in these daily battles it was not a matter for pride:

> When we live in community [sisters], let us choose obedience over discipline; for the latter teaches arrogance, while the former calls for humility.[16]

Making a name for yourself as a famous ascetic, or looking down on others who have given up less, is to miss the point of the religious life. Discipline is good, but obedience is better, because it overcomes the last and most pernicious of the Eight Thoughts outlined by Evagrius, that is the sin of pride.

Always, the underlying motivation for action must be closely scrutinized. Too often the right thing can be done for the wrong reason. It may be right, on occasion, to modify one's ascetic commitments, rather than build up too much stress in the body and mind, as we saw in the Introduction—a bow should not be stretched too taut or it may snap or injure the one who pulls back the string. On the other hand, a ship doesn't turn back in the face of the first contrary wind; rather the captain may cause the ship to tack, to turn into the wind and allow a forward progress by degrees, turning now with, now against the wind, making slow but steady progress in a contrary way through the sea. Syncletica continues with her nautical imagery:

> Are you fasting? Do not use illness as a pretext [to stop]. Actually, those who are not fasting fall victim to the same diseases.

> Have you made a start in the virtuous life? Do not bolt when the Enemy checks you; for he himself is confounded by your steadfastness. Those who are beginning a sea voyage first encounter a favoring wind when they have unfurled their sails, but later a contrary wind blows against them; the sailors, however, do not dock the ship on account of a fortuitous breeze, but they continue their voyage after lying quiet for a little while or even after having battled against the storm blast. So we too shall complete our voyage successfully when we encounter an opposing wind, if we raise the cross in place of the sail.[17]

All is done by the strength of the cross of Christ, the one who stilled the storm on the lake of Galilee, and who showed no fear of the raging waters when the disciples were terrified half to death. Syncletica likewise shows an impressive absence of fear. She must have been an inspiring spiritual guide. Like the sixteenth-century Saint Teresa of Avila in her book *The Way of Perfection*, Syncletica tells her sisters not to grow fainthearted in their spiritual life. "Don't give up going to the chapel to say your prayers just because you have a headache!" says Teresa. "Don't stop fasting just because you are hungry," says Syncletica; "People get sick whether or not they fast—don't think you'll be safe huddled away in your own room! Rather, be like the sailors who have weathered many storms in their lives, who bear the scars of swinging sails and flailing ropes. Set a steady course and the haven you long for will soon come into view."

Sisters and Brothers

Despite the commonality of the teaching by the desert fathers and mothers, there was little direct contact between female and male monastics. One story in the thematic collection of sayings of the desert elders, under the theme of self-control, reveals something of the tensions between the two groups:

> Once a brother went to visit his sister who was ill in a nunnery. She was someone of great faith. She herself had never agreed to

> see a man nor did she want to give her brother occasion for coming into the company of women. She commanded him, 'Go away, my brother, and pray for me, for by Christ's grace I shall see you in the kingdom of heaven.'[18]

The sister gives up her natural desire to see her brother for the sake of protecting his vocation as a monk. It seems his sense of calling is more fragile than hers. Another saying immediately follows in the text:

> On a journey a monk met some nuns and when he saw them he turned aside off the road. The abbess said to him, 'If you had been a true monk, you would not have looked to see that we are women.'[19]

Why would the monk not have noticed that they were women? Was it because he would have been lost in prayer, keeping his gaze on the ground to avoid distraction, and maintaining an unceasing watch over his thoughts? Or was it perhaps that he had gone beyond the distinctions of male and female, and like St. Paul, realized their essential unity in Christ? Was he able to truly say: "There is no longer Jew or Greek, there is no longer slave or free, there is no longer male and female; for all of you are one in Christ Jesus" (Gal 3:28).

Another story from the desert tradition describes a similar meeting on the road. Once a group of monks were on a journey and met a group of women, one of whom resolutely looked the head monk in the eye. "Why do you look at me when your eyes should be cast down at your feet?" the monk asked. The woman replied, "It is said that Adam was formed from the dust of the earth, so it is right for you to look down to the earth, but Eve was formed from Adam, so in looking at you I am reminded of the work of my creator!"

Sometimes the rivalry between monastics crosses over into what would seem to be an example of misogyny:

> Another time, two old men, great anchorites, came to the district of Pelusia to visit Amma Sarah. When they arrived one said to the other, 'Let us humiliate this old woman.' So they said to her,

> 'Be careful not to become conceited thinking to yourself: "Look how anchorites are coming to see me, a mere woman."' But Amma Sarah said to them, 'According to nature I am a woman, but not according to my thoughts' . . . She also said to the brothers, 'It is I who am a man, you who are women.'[20]

Perhaps it is a matter of translation—"Let us humiliate . . ." is not quite the same as "let us teach humility . . ." If the latter were truly the intention then no doubt the same harsh treatment would have been meted out to all, regardless of sex. But Sarah is no novice in this life, and has no need of the instruction of these self-appointed teachers of the Way. So, Sarah has the last laugh after all; and yet it is sad that she could only do so by calling herself a man. In the ancient world, women were considered to be lesser creatures than men, the female being an incompletely formed male. To call a woman "manly" was seen as a compliment; "womanly" meant being too dependent on emotions rather than having a clear, logical mind. Much was made of the Genesis account of the Fall of humanity, which was blamed on Eve as the first to heed the devil's temptation and eat from the tree of life.

Although the quick wit of the women in these stories can be celebrated, still it was not often that women and men renunciates were in each other's company. At the very beginning there were mixed communities of men and women in Egypt, but it wasn't long before such foundations were outlawed by church authorities. In their stead there was only the possibility of "double monasteries"—communities of both sexes on the same site and perhaps worshipping together, led by a man or a woman—or parallel monasteries with little contact between monks and nuns.

The attempt to avoid all contact with women was sometimes taken to extremes:

> On a journey, a brother had with him his old mother. They came to a river, and the old woman could not get across. Her son took off his cloak, and wrapped it round his hands, so as not to touch his mother's body and carried her across the river. His mother said to him, 'Why did you wrap up your hands like that, my

> son?' He said, 'Because a woman's body is fire. Simply because I was touching you, the memory of other women might come in to my mind.'[21]

A simple question arises in response to this story: Where was the fire? In the mother's body, or in the mind of her son? And yet at least the two felt able to go on a journey together. An old Zen story is often told in monasteries in the far East: two monks were travelling together and came to a swollen river, meeting a woman unable to cross. One monk avoided the woman and waded across himself; the other picked up the woman and carried her across without a further thought. Later that day the first monk asked the second, "Why did you touch that woman when we are monks?" To which the second replied, "I only carried her across the river. You have been carrying her in your mind all day long!"

The Christian monks of the desert carried women (and men) in their memories also. They liked to retell stories about famous courtesans who repented of their profession and became ascetics in the desert. These women either disguised themselves as monks (even rising to become abbot of a monastery), or lived in total seclusion, such that their clothes disintegrated, and their hair grew long to keep their modesty. Their model was the biblical figure of Mary of Bethany, often identified as Mary Magdalene, a repentant sinner as told by St. Luke's Gospel. Well-known among these women were St. Mary of Egypt, Pelagia and Thais, although the details of their legends tended to get confused.[22] Perhaps the monks got carried away themselves in their retelling of these tales.

The redoubtable Syncletica would have none of it:

> The holy Syncletica said: 'We who have chosen this holy way of life ought above all to preserve chastity. Even among men of the world chastity is highly regarded. But in the world they are also stupid about it, and sin with their other senses. For they peep indecently, and laugh immoderately.'[23]

Perhaps not only in the world. In any case, Syncletica is remarkably practical and writes the usual prescription as a cure for lust:

> 'Bodily poison is cured by still stronger antidotes; so fasting and prayer drive out sordid temptation from us.' She also said, 'The pleasures and riches of the world must not attract you as if they were of any use to you. Because of its pleasure the art of cooking is respected, but by rigorous fasting you should trample on this pleasure. Never have enough bread to satisfy you and do not long for wine.'[24]

Syncletica is speaking here as a desert ascetic, not the wife and mother of an earthly family. She is one who recognizes the pleasures of food and dining together drinking fine wines, but she will not stay in the kitchen herself. She sets her mind firmly on other pleasures beyond those of this fleeting world.

Once again, Syncletica returns to her feminine imagery, referring to the womb as an example of the life now led in expectancy, waiting for the fulfilment of eternal life when we are born again:

> Whatever we do or gain in this world, let us consider it insignificant in comparison to the eternal wealth that is to come. We are on this earth as if in a second maternal womb. In that inner recess we did not have a life such as we have here, for we did not have there solid nourishment such as we enjoy now, nor were we able to be active, indeed, as we are here, and we in fact existed without the light of the sun and of any glimmer of light. Just as, then, when we were in that inner chamber, we did without many of the things of this world, so also in the present world we are impoverished in comparison with the kingdom of heaven. We have sampled the nourishment here; let us reach for the Divine! We have enjoyed the light in this world; let us long for the sun of righteousness! Let us regard the heavenly Jerusalem as our homeland and our mother, and let us call God our father. Let us live prudently in this world that we may obtain eternal life.[25]

The earth is a womb of expectancy, a shelter in the storm before sailing out to new horizons. Like the embryo within, the comfort of the dark must be left behind if the radiant light of the kingdom of heaven is to be enjoyed. God and God's Kingdom are imaged in a balance of feminine and masculine terms. Birth is a parable for the rebirth from above, as Jesus taught Nicodemus (see John 3). Our true home and mother's embrace is near says Amma Syncletica—let us reach out, open our eyes, and see.

Questions for reflection and discussion

- Who are the most influential religious women in the world today?
- Are there particular women who have inspired you in your journey of faith?
- What would the world look like if the majority of faith leaders were women?

Further reading

Laura Swan, 2001, *The Forgotten Desert Mothers: Sayings, Lives and Stories of Early Christian Women*, New York: Paulist Press.

Benedicta Ward SLG, 1987, *Harlots of the Desert: A Study of Repentance in Early Monastic Sources*, Cistercian Studies Series, Collegeville, MN: Cistercian Publications.

Benedicta Ward SLG, 1975/1984 revd edn, *The Sayings of the Desert Fathers: The Alphabetical Collection*, Collegeville, MN: Cistercian Publications.

Notes

1 Robert T. Meyer, 1964, *Palladius: The Lausiac History*, Ancient Christian Writers, New York: Paulist Press, p. 37.

2 Meyer, *Palladius*, p. 95.

3 Philip Rousseau, 1999, *Pachomius: The Making of a Community in Fourth-Century Egypt*, Berkeley, CA: University of California Press, pp. 146–7.

4 Meyer, *Palladius*, pp. 136–7.

5 Meyer, *Palladius*, pp. 145–6.

6 Benedicta Ward SLG, 1975/1984 revd edn, *The Sayings of the Desert Fathers: The Alphabetical Collection*, Collegeville, MN: Cistercian Publications, p. 83.

7 Laura Swan, 2001, *The Forgotten Desert Mothers: Sayings, Lives and Stories of Early Christian Women*, New York: Paulist Press, p. 65.

8 Swan, *Forgotten Desert Mothers*, p. 67.

9 Ward, *Alphabetical Collection*, p. 84.

10 Ward, *Alphabetical Collection*, pp. 230–1.

11 Ward, *Alphabetical Collection*, p. 231.

12 Pseudo-Athanasius, 2003, *The Life & Regimen of the Blessed & Holy Syncletica, Part 1, The Translation*, by Elizabeth Bryson Bongie, Eugene, OR: Wipf & Stock, p. 30.

13 Pseudo-Athanasius, *Holy Syncletica*, pp. 31–2.

14 Pseudo-Athanasius, *Holy Syncletica*, p. 32.

15 Pseudo-Athanasius, *Holy Syncletica*, p. 55.

16 Pseudo-Athanasius, *Holy Syncletica*, p. 61.

17 Pseudo-Athanasius, *Holy Syncletica*, pp. 62–3.

18 Benedicta Ward, 2003, *The Desert Fathers: Sayings of the Early Christian Monks*, London: Penguin Books, p. 30.

19 Ward, *Desert Fathers*, p. 30.

20 Ward, *Alphabetical Collection*, p. 230.

21 Ward, *Desert Fathers*, p. 31.

22 See Benedicta Ward, 1987, *Harlots of the Desert: A Study of Repentance in Early Monastic Sources*, Collegeville, MN: Cistercian Publications.

23 Ward, *Desert Fathers*, p. 27.

24 Ward, *Desert Fathers*, p. 27.

25 Pseudo-Athanasius, *Holy Syncletica*, p. 56.

3

Macarius, Diadochus and the Comfort of the Holy Spirit

> The soul that is deemed to be judged worthy to participate in the light of the Holy Spirit by becoming his throne and habitation . . . becomes all light, all face, all eye. There is no part of the soul that is not full of the spiritual eyes of light.[1]

One of the teachers of Evagrius was a hermit monk known as Macarius of Egypt (c. 300–391). As a young man he had married at the request of his family, but was soon widowed when his wife contracted a fever and died. At the age of 30, after his parents had also died, he left his hometown to become a monk, learning the ascetic life from a hermit who lived nearby. His fame as a holy man quickly spread, but some tried to undermine his reputation. One story concerning him tells of a young woman who falsely accused him of being the father of her unborn child. Rather than try to defend himself, Macarius responded to the accusation with silence, and gave the money he earned weaving baskets to the pregnant woman, saying to himself, "Macarius, it seems you have found yourself a wife!" After a difficult labor the woman confessed to wrongly traducing the innocence of Macarius, and the child was safely born.

Macarius was well aware of the difficulties of raising a child, as shown in a response he made to a penitent monk seeking his advice:

> It is written, my child, 'I do not desire the death of a sinner so much as his repentance and his life' [Ezek. 33.11]. Repent, therefore, my child; you will see him who is gentle, our Lord Jesus Christ, his face full of joy for you, like a nursing mother whose

> face is full of joy for her child. When he raises his hands and his face up to her, even if he is full of all kinds of uncleanness, she does not turn away from that bad smell and excrement but takes pity on him and lifts him up and presses him to her breast, her face full of joy, and everything about him is sweet to her. If, then, this created person has pity for her child, how much greater is the love of the creator, our Lord Jesus Christ, for us![2]

Like Julian of Norwich in fourteenth-century England, Macarius was aware of the motherly compassion of God, and had no illusions about the perils of parenthood. But he knew his path was different—God was calling him to renounce family life and instead to search for God in a wilderness both physical and emotional.

Eventually, Macarius became an ascetic living at the monastic settlement of Nitria in Upper Egypt. He spent some time with Antony the Great, and he himself became known as "Macarius the Great" and "Macarius the Spirit-bearer," being sought out for his discernment of spirits, and the wise advice he gave to those who came to him for counsel. When Antony died Macarius inherited his staff as a token of the regard in which he was held by the older man. Macarius was known as "the young elder," a man with an old head on young shoulders, as the saying goes. It was said of him that his face shone at night, like the face of Moses as he descended Mount Sinai, after receiving the tablets of the Law from the hands of God. As a result, Macarius was known as "the glowing lantern," and the monastery founded in his name became known as "the glowing monastery." It is still inhabited today by monks of the Coptic Church in Egypt.

In his classic text *Praktikos*, Evagrius witnessed to the rigorous yet compassionate attitude Macarius had towards his body:

> Our holy and most ascetic master [Macarius the Great] stated that the monk should always live as if he were to die on the morrow but at the same time that he should treat his body as if he were to live on with it for many years to come. For, he said, by the first attitude he will be able to cut off every thought that comes from *acedia* and thus become more fervent in his monastic

> practices, by the second device he will preserve his body in good health and maintain its continence intact.[3]

Macarius was a very prudent teacher, in the tradition of his own teacher Antony, who didn't want to overstretch his disciples. A keen ambition is one thing, but to be in too much of a hurry in the monastic life can cause problems later on. Like many ascetics he was probably harder on himself than on his disciples, not wanting to overburden them by too high an ideal. And yet he had reached this state of equanimity himself only by strict self-discipline. Perhaps this is the paradox of the religious life—every ounce of energy must be spent, so that one finally realizes that nothing is achieved by one's own efforts. All is grace and peace, the work is just in clearing away whatever obscures that grace, to reveal that which has always been present—the radiant goodness of the Lord.

Macarius also taught that prayer should be as simple as possible. When asked how one should pray, he said:

> There is no need at all to make long discourses; it is enough to stretch out one's hands and say, 'Lord, as you will, and as you know, have mercy.' And if the conflict grows fiercer say, 'Lord, help!' He knows very well what we need and he shows us his mercy.[4]

Here we see one of the first instances of "monologistic prayer," that is, prayer of only a few words, if not just one. Such sentences are found in many places of Scripture, expressing a simple heartfelt need, as described in Psalm 130:1: "Out of the depths I cry to you, Lord. Lord, hear my voice! Let your ears be attentive to the voice of my supplications!" This kind of prayer usually consists of a single exclamation or a cry for mercy, frequently recited in private devotions or in daily liturgical prayers. One such was Psalm 51, a psalm that was numbered among the "seven penitential psalms" by Cassiodorus' commentary of the sixth century, and which begins: "Have mercy on me, O God, according to your steadfast love." Abba Isaiah, as recorded by John Cassian (360–435) in the tenth book of his monastic *Conferences*, speaks at length of the ceaseless repetition of a verse from the Psalms. The verse he recommended was: "Be pleased, O God, to deliver me. O Lord, make haste to help me!" (Ps 70:1). This practice was adopted by Benedict of Nursia in his Rule, being enshrined in the opening versicle and response at each gathering for communal prayer.

In the Gospel of Luke, Jesus describes a similar practice in the parable of the two men praying in the temple, where the one who goes to his home in a right relationship with God says only and repeatedly: "God, be merciful to me, a sinner!" (Luke 18:13). In John's Gospel we read of the short acclamations of disciples of the risen Lord: Mary's cry "Rabbouni!" to the one she had mistaken for a gardener, or Thomas' sudden realization as he stood before Jesus: "My Lord and my God!" (John 20:16, 28). In their scriptural context these verses from the Gospel of John were single unrepeated exclamations, but they could be adapted to become almost continuous prayers, like the medieval repetition of the Lord's Prayer, aided by a set of rosary beads, known as a *paternoster*. Mary's cry "Rabbouni!" echoes the call of Jesus to his heavenly father in the Aramaic word, "*Abwoon!*" And from the above encounter of Thomas with the risen Lord, a thousand years later St. Francis of Assisi learned to repeat in prayer the phrase, "My God and my All!" Just hearing this form of devotion on the lips of Francis converted his first follower, Brother Bernard, and so the Franciscans became a community rooted in monologistic prayer.

The essence of such prayer is the continuous repetition of the chosen word or phrase, hence the importance of manual work in the religious life, during which the prayer can be said silently or quietly as the practitioner completes the work at hand. In this way the mind is attuned to a constant awareness of the presence of God and to the ever-deepening realization of the need for God's mercy in every situation of life.

In the Egyptian wilderness of the fourth century, Macarius also showed himself adept at brevity, both in his prayers as well as in his teaching. As an old man he once ended a talk he had given to the monks gathered around him, saying: "Flee, my brothers!" To which one of them replied, "We have already fled to the desert. Where else should we go?" Looking round at the expectant faces of his friends Macarius simply lifted up his finger, touched his lips, and said, "Flee this!" Then he left them in a swirl of sand, went back to his cell, and sat down to pray. To the end, Macarius retained a depth of humility, as shown in another of his sayings. The story goes that one day when he was praying in his cell, a voice whispered in his ear, "Macarius, you have not yet attained the level of two women living in a certain village far from here." Intrigued, Macarius rose early the next day, took his staff and set off on a journey to find the women. Being guided by an angel he found the place and was warmly received. After their greetings Macarius asked the two women, "I have travelled a long way to visit you here—tell me, what is your way of life?" Wanting to maintain their humility, they asked him why he should have taken all this trouble to meet them. To this, he replied, "Don't worry about that. I was sent by God; that is enough." So, they told him their story. "For 15 years we have lived together in this house without speaking an idle word to each other. We both implored our husbands to allow us to live as nuns, but they would not allow us to do so. Instead, we made an agreement with God that we would live together in peace, directing our thoughts and prayers to God and the saints, and devote ourselves to unceasing prayer, fasting and good works."

The story concludes with the response of Macarius the Spirit-bearer:

> 'Truly, it is not the name of "monk" or "layperson" or "virgin" or "wife and husband" but an upright disposition that God seeks, and he gives his Holy Spirit to all of these people.' And after the old man had profited from meeting the two women, he returned to his cell, clapping his hands and saying, 'I have not been at peace with my brothers like these lay women have with one another.'[5]

The *Macarian Homilies*

Beginning with an exposition of the vision of the throne of God, as recorded in the first chapter of the prophecy of Ezekiel, an unknown author of the late fourth century wrote a series of 50 homilies in the name of Macarius the Great. The use of pseudonyms, rather shocking to our modern abhorrence of plagiarism, was widespread in ancient Judaism and Christianity. Biblical examples include the ascription of the Pentateuch, the first five books of the Bible, to Moses; the Psalms to David; Proverbs and Wisdom to Solomon; and numerous letters of the New Testament to Paul, Peter or John. Perhaps the most well-known and influential non-biblical pseudonymous work was the short treatise, *The Mystical Theology*, which was ascribed to Paul's convert at the Athenian Areopagus, by the name of Dionysius, though it was probably written by a Syrian monk centuries later. Scholars tend to give such works the additional title "Pseudo"—as in Pseudo-Dionysius or Pseudo-Macarius. Although there is an element of subterfuge in this practice, perhaps being used to assert the orthodoxy of an unauthorized work, it doesn't necessarily mean that the real author was trying to hide their assumed identity. In part it was a compliment to the revered figure of the past, as if the author were seeking to write in the style of the one whose name they have borrowed, to declare themselves as a disciple, or even to "channel" the spirit of the original author.

The *Macarian Homilies* is one such work, written as if by Macarius the Great of Egypt, but due to its Syrian imagery and vocabulary more likely to have been penned by a monk or nun in the region of Syria or Mesopotamia in the late fourth century. These texts explore themes found also in the charismatic movement of the day known as "Messalianism." This was something of a reaction against the authority structures of the church at the time. It stressed the importance of personal experience in religion, through the practice of continuous prayer, and downplayed the sacraments of the established church. Women were given a higher status than in the official ecclesiastical structures. Of particular note is the warm, vibrant faith which flows out of these writings, describing intimate experiences of the Holy Spirit, particularly of the radiant light perceived in and around those imbued with holiness. While not being seen as a document directly produced by the Messalians, still the *Macarian Homilies* lean in that direction, perhaps being a mollifying reaction to the more extreme critics of the Messalian movement. Whatever their provenance, these homilies have long been a favorite among Christians, not least among the Franciscans of the thirteenth century in Italy, and the post-Reformation pietist movements of Germany and England. John Wesley, for example, wrote in his diary for 30 June 1736, "I read Macarius and sang!"[6]

While having wonderful flights of devotion, and visions of the celestial throne of God, the *Homilies* begin with their feet on the ground:

> The true foundation of prayer is this: to be very vigilant over thoughts and to pray in much tranquillity and peace in order not to be a source of offence to others . . . A person ought to labour to concentrate on their thoughts. They must cut away all underlying matter that leads to evil thoughts, urging themselves towards God. They should not allow their thoughts to control their will, but they need to collect them whenever they wander off in all directions, discerning natural thoughts from those that are evil. The soul, being tainted by sin, is similar to a large forest on a mountain, or like reeds in a river, or like thick, thorny bushes. Whoever passes through such a place needs to hold out their hands before them and with force and labour push aside whatever lies in their path. So also the thoughts that come from the adverse power beset the soul. Therefore, there is need for great diligence and mental alertness so that one may distinguish those outside thoughts that rise by the power of the adversary.[7]

This is a teaching firmly in the tradition of Evagrius and the practice of watchfulness and vigilance regarding the wayward thoughts that beset the mind. It is seen as a struggle with demons, wrestling in a metaphorical darkness in which the soul is lost in its passions. This form of prayer takes as its basis New Testament texts such as St Paul's exhortation to the Corinthians, "we take every thought captive to obey Christ" (2 Cor 10:5). Although this verse can be interpreted as referring to the struggle of the Christian missionary with the pagan religions and Greek philosophical structures of thought, Macarius sees it more as a battle with the passions of greed, anger and pride. By this diligent struggle, "anyone united to the Lord becomes one spirit with him" (1 Cor 6:17), as Macarius says in *Homily Nine*.[8] In this way the person of prayer knows by their own experience which is the more nourishing to the soul—the thoughts that come from the Spirit of God, or those that originate with the Adversary.

Brothers and sisters

In this struggle the Christian is not alone, but is surrounded by brothers and sisters who encourage one another out of their mutual love and service. Macarius says in *Homily Three*:

> The brethren should conduct themselves toward one another with the greatest love, whether in praying or reading Scripture or doing any kind of work so that they may have the foundation of charity towards others. And thus their various tasks or undertakings may find approval with those who pray and those who read and those who work; all can conduct themselves toward each other in sincerity and simplicity to their mutual profit.[9]

Whatever task be undertaken by each brother or sister, all should be regarded as an offering of love for the welfare of all. Everything is shared, even the blessings of ministry. This is a good way to avoid individual egotistical pride—a practice as important for a hermit as for a cenobite living in community. Macarius goes on to describe the monastic life as "angelic"—a typical theme of that time. It is based on the saying of Jesus in the Gospels:

> Jesus said to the disciples, "Those who belong to this age marry and are given in marriage; but those who are considered worthy of a place in that age and in the resurrection from the dead neither marry nor are given in marriage. Indeed they cannot die any more, because they are like angels and are children of God, being children of the resurrection." (Luke 20:34-36)

In Luke's version of this saying of Jesus it is implied that not only is there no marriage in heaven, but those who are entering the

Kingdom of God do not marry in this life either, for they are already like angels. This is known as the "encratic" tendency in Luke's writings, and in other early Christian texts such as the Gospel of Thomas. It refers to a tendency to emphasize the importance of celibacy, from the Greek word *enkrateia* (*ἐγκράτεια*) meaning "self-controlled," a fruit of the Spirit mentioned in Galatians 5:22-23.

Such an emphasis on the calling of Christians to live an "angelic" life, as in the writings of Macarius and others, is perhaps a pious exaggeration when applied to the religious communities of the day and through the centuries. Not many monks and nuns are angelic in all their ways! Nonetheless it was a teaching not dissimilar to that of St. Paul in his First Letter to the Corinthians (7:1-16), where he encourages Christians to focus their energies on the greatest need of the times. Such an attitude was based on the nature of the coming tribulations, which Paul and others took to mean the end of all things in their own lifetime, and the inauguration of the imminent Kingdom of God. Monasticism and the celibate calling was in part a response to that sense of urgency. There was no time to get married and raise children—the end was nigh.

And yet the emphasis here in the *Macarian Homilies* is not so much on the urgency of the End Times as on the simple love and kindness that all should show each other, regardless of marital status or eschatological belief. Such a life together contained the balanced practice of prayer, study and work, each of which was done as a way of service of their fellow Christians:

> The brethren, therefore, regardless of what work they are doing, ought to conduct themselves toward each other in love and cheerfulness. And the one who works should say of the one who is praying: 'I also possess the treasure which my brother possesses since it is common.' And let him who prays say of him who reads: 'What he gains from reading redounds also to my advantage.' And he who works let him thus say: 'The work which I am doing is for the common good.' For as the members of the body, being many, are one body (1 Cor. 12.12) and help each other while each still performs its own function.[10]

Prayer is the foundation of all things, but the benefit of all activity is shared out equally among all. If one reads a book, it is not just for personal entertainment but for mutual enrichment, increasing the understanding of the gospel among all members of the community. If another works, that is labor which leads to good health and well-being for all. If one prays, all benefit. This is true spiritual communism, sharing not just the material goods of this life, but realizing that all spiritual benefits must be shared if they are to be of help not just to oneself but to all. Macarius, following the above passage, mentions one member of the community devoting themselves to prayer for six hours at a time. This is not a common experience, then or now, though in contemplative monasteries some may pray in this way in the quiet of the night. But such dedication is not strictly necessary according to Macarius. Although one may give themselves to prayer alone, another may be occupied in work so that he can only sit down to pray for an hour at a time. Nonetheless, while performing his or her tasks:

> The interior man is caught up in prayer and plunged into the infinite depths of that other world with great sweetness. His whole mind as a result is lifted up and caught up in that region where he sojourns. In that time his thoughts of earthly cares recede into oblivion because now his thoughts are filled and held captivated by divine and heavenly things . . . and [he] says: 'Would that my soul might pass over with my prayer!'[11]

The flame of the Spirit

According to "Macarius," when the Spirit of God inflames the heart in this way it is as if the heart itself would burst. Sometimes the flames burn strongly; at other times the flames die down gently and slowly but without being finally extinguished. This is the life of grace as experienced in the communities of which Macarius was a leader. But then in his homilies he becomes more personal, and starts to speak of the experiences of 'certain persons' when it seems clear that, reading between the lines, this is really the experience of the author himself. Like St. Paul speaking of a man being caught up to the third heaven (2 Cor 12:2), this is really a piece of bold spiritual autobiography:

> To certain persons the sign of the cross appeared as light and plunged itself deep into the inner person. At another time a man, while praying, was thrown into a trance. He found himself standing in church before the altar . . . To others at times there appeared a splendid robe, such as not found anywhere in the whole world, not made by human hands . . . brilliant like lightning . . . Sometimes indeed the very light itself, shining in the heart, opened up interiorly and in a profound way a hidden light, so that the whole person was completely drowned with that sweet contemplation . . . overwhelmed was he by the excessive love and sweetness of the hidden mysteries that were being revealed to him. The result was that the person was granted liberty and arrived at a degree of purity and freedom from sin.[12]

Already an orthodox reader would hear warning bells ringing. The author, by virtue of the light that suffuses his mind, is transported to an altar in a church (regardless of the invitation of bishops!), or dressed in resplendent robes radiating light as if he were himself transfigured on the holy mountain with (or as?) Christ. Finally, he experiences "a degree of purity and freedom from sin" (without the sacramental mediation of a priest to offer absolution!) The reader can see how the church authorities might get nervous. This was the kind of writing that would later inspire the Cathars in thirteenth-century France, and eventually led to their brutal suppression by the Inquisition and the troops of those loyal to the established church.

But these homilies describe a beautiful set of visions envisaging a new earth, where people dwell in harmony, and door after door is opened, revealing more and more the all-inclusive love of God. Everyone has a home here, everyone has a dwelling place in richer and richer mansions, resting places beyond human telling, where the "I" of the author is finally set free to proclaim the truth of his visions:

> After I received the experience of the sign of the cross, grace now acts in this manner. It quiets all my parts and my heart so that

> the soul with the greatest joy seems to be a guileless child. No longer am I a man that condemns Greek or Jew or sinner or worldling. Truly, the interior person looks on all human beings with pure eyes and finds joy in the whole world. He really wishes to reverence and love all Greeks and Jews.[13]

In response, the homilist finds himself in floods of tears, weeping over the whole human race. The Spirit urges him to reconcile all people in love and joy and peace, without distinction or favoritism. At other times he rests in silence and tranquility, in ineffable rest and well-being. At such times no word can be uttered, for all language falls short of the splendor revealed within the heart. Everything leads to an ecstatic finale celebrating the all-consuming love of God:

> Finally, when a person reaches the perfection of the Spirit, completely purified of all passions and united to and interpenetrated by the Paraclete Spirit in an ineffable communion, and is deemed worthy to become spirit in mutual penetration with the Spirit, then it becomes all light, all eye, all spirit, all joy, all repose, all happiness, all love, all compassion, all goodness and kindness.[14]

The author becomes like one of the angels in the nearer presence of God: cherubim and seraphim who are all eye, all awareness, never losing the sight or love of God, never ceasing to share that love with others. This is a religion of visions and the spiritual senses. Do they really see God, or the blazing splendor of God, as described in the almost psychedelic vision of "the appearance of the likeness of the glory of the Lord" (Ezek 1:28)? Whatever they see, it is a vision and a prophecy that unites them to each other and to God. As Moses says to the Israelites: "Would that all the Lord's people were prophets, and that the Lord would put his spirit on them!" (Num 11:29).

Diadochus of Photike

Diadochus, Bishop of Photike, a rugged, mountainous region in the north-west of Greece, is a figure largely unknown in the history of

Christian spirituality. We know next to nothing about him, other than that he was the author of several treatises on the theological issues of his day, of which only a few remain. His most important work, a *Century of Gnostic Chapters*, comprising a hundred short reflections and meditations, was influential on later more well-known writers such as Maximus the Confessor and Nicodemus of the Holy Mountain. He writes against the background of the Messalian movement discussed above, in relation to the *Macarian Homilies.*

One of the chief teachings of Diadochus was of the importance of baptism—a sacrament not mentioned by Evagrius, and downplayed by the Messalians. Diadochus, in contrast, wrote that from the very moment of baptism, grace is hidden deep within the soul, working secretly to restore the image and likeness of God in humanity. This is revealed by the operation of the "spiritual sense" (*αἴσθησἴς νοῦς/aisthesis nous*), an awareness that unites a mind dissipated by the five bodily senses, and which directly perceives the workings of God's love. It is an unbroken recollection of the presence of God, facilitated by constantly calling out the divine name "Lord Jesus!" In this use of the name of Jesus as a monologistic prayer, Diadochus is bringing us one step nearer the full expression of hesychasm, the prayer of silence, in the Christian church. Andrew Louth points to the importance of Diadochus in the history of mystical theology:

> In Diadochus we find a uniting of the two traditions that come from the fourth century monastic milieu, that of Evagrius and that ascribed to Macarius. It is not being claimed that Diadochus is typical of the East. There is a constant tension in Eastern mystical theology between Evagrianism and Messalianism . . . Diadochus simply provides us with an example of how these two, apparently so diverse, traditions could converge.[15]

It could be said that in Diadochus we find one of the earliest examples of the reconciliation of the intellectual and the emotional, the head and the heart, as represented by Evagrius and Macarius respectively. As ever in the history of ideas, the reality is not quite so clear-cut, as we will see as we go further into the teaching of Diadochus, and outline his antecedents and successors. For example,

Evagrius the intellectual often talks of the importance of love, and the empathetic *Macarian Homilies* are clearly expounded meditations on the transformation of the mind by the Spirit. Although there is enough truth in the comparison of the two elements of intellect and emotion to illustrate their necessary combination, it may not be the best way to proceed. The journey into awestruck silence in the conscious presence of God is not easy; it requires all the strength and endurance that we can muster, all the faculties and gifts that God bestows on us along the way. Dichotomies such as head/heart or soul/body are not necessarily helpful if they lead to an internal division that inhibits spiritual energy like a psychotherapeutic block. Dualities all too easily collapse into seeing one side of the equation as good and the other as bad. This has demonstratively happened in the Platonic Christian tradition by the praise of the soul and the denigration of the body, leading to an unhealthy rejection of physicality and a reliance only on what is "pure" or "spiritual." In the hesychastic tradition, the term "heart" is a unifying designation referring to thoughts as well as emotions, the center of human personhood. It is that into which the love of God is poured through the Holy Spirit (Rom 5:5), as well as the place of our thoughts and intentions, to be skillfully discerned by the word of God (Heb 4:12). The heart and its intuitions are essential allies on the spiritual path.

The Sense of the heart

Discernment, another watchword of the hesychast tradition, requires the use of all the senses, spiritual as well as physical. True hesychastic silence is not a blankness, a dulling of perception or a loss of awareness. Rather it is a heightening of perception, a filtering out of the grime in our thoughts so that the depths of the stream of consciousness come into a much clearer vision.

Diadochus leads us into an exploration of the spiritual senses:

> Whoever loves God in the Sense of the heart [Greek: *αἴσθησῐς καρδίας/aisthesis kardias*], this man has been perceived by him; for one comes to live in love for God to the same extent that one

> receives the love of God in the Sense of the soul [*αἴσθησίς ψυχῆς*/ *aisthesis psyches*]. So thereafter such a person will not desist from reaching out for the illumination of perception in excessive yearning, to the point of sensing from that Sense which is of one's bones, no longer aware of himself, but rather being entirely transformed by love for God. Such a person both is and is not present in this life, for while still dwelling in his body he journeys ceaselessly to God through love in the movement of the soul. From then on, his heart being kindled through the fire of love, he unyieldingly clings to God by an imperative of longing, being simply taken up from affection for himself by love for God. For 'if we have been taken up,' it says 'it was for God, but if we are in our right mind, it is for you' (2 Cor. 5.13).[16]

Here Diadochus sums up much of his teaching. He uses various terms to point to his central concern with spiritual perception: "the Sense of the Heart," "the Sense of the Soul," "the Sense of one's bones," all of which are used of the one overriding perception of the influence of God in the inmost depths of the person. As noted above, "heart" is neither intellectual nor emotional, it is simply personal. It is the place from which we emerge as we relate to the world and to God, the focus of our personal and corporate being. It is also intrinsically linked with the body, here reflected in talk of the Sense of the bones. It is about our gut feelings, our intuition, our most immediate perceptions. The body is the vehicle of our union with God, the transport of love by the "imperative of longing." The saying of Paul translated here as "if we have been taken up," is a difficult verse to translate. It could mean something like: "if we are beside ourselves with concern for you . . ." in terms of their ongoing friendship. Diadochus, however, seems to take it as pointing to a direct spiritual experience of the love of God: if he is totally absorbed in silent (hesychastic) prayer then that is for the sake of God's glory, but if he is absorbed in worldly concerns for his fellow Christians that that is for the sake of his Corinthian believers.

Diadochus continues to elucidate his experience of the Spirit:

> Whenever anyone begins to sense love for God abundantly, then he begins to love his neighbour also by the Sense of the Spirit [*αἴσθησις πνεύματός/aisthesis pneumatos*]; for this is the love which all the Scriptures expound. The affection which is according to the flesh is all too easily dissolved when any slight pretext is found, since it has not been bound by the Sense of the Spirit; whereas even if it might happen that some provocation comes upon the soul activated by God, the bond of love is not loosened within it, since immediately rekindling itself in the direction of the good by the ardour of its love for God, it again summons up love of neighbour with great joy, even if it was greatly insulted or injured by him. For the soul activated by God consumes the bitterness of the quarrel absolutely by means of the sweetness of God.[17]

Any discovery of the love of God automatically leads to a more abundant love of one's neighbour. Diadochus is keenly aware of how fragile human relationships are, how quickly human affection turns to disaffection, how easily love turns to hate on the level of ordinary relations. But things need not be so: the Sense of the Spirit, so important to Macarius, is an ever-present resource of spiritual awareness, of perception of the need in everyone to love and be loved, and of the mistaken paths we follow thinking that our happiness can somehow be separated from that of others.

This theme of clear awareness, purity of heart, is linked, as so often in this tradition, with the perception of an inner light:

> One must not doubt that when the intellect begins to be activated constantly by the divine light it becomes a transparent whole, so that it sees its own light abundantly; for this comes to be expressed whenever the power of the soul masters the passions.[18]

This light is what radiates from the saints, makes them in every sense luminous people, shining from the core of their being. It is a theme that we will return to, particularly in writers such as Simeon the New Theologian. It is linked to the sense of transparency, a complete lack of guile, that others may see obliquely and that we ourselves may discover within our own heart as we search for the radiant Spirit of a clear mind (*νοῦς/nous*).

Bodies and the Spirit

Although Diadochus talks about eventually leaving the body behind in the spiritual quest, nonetheless the body itself is not an enemy but a partner of the soul:

> Eating and drinking while giving thanks to God for what has been set before you or mixed is in no way contrary to the rule of knowledge, since everything is very good. But voluntarily abstaining from what is enjoyable and abundant is constitutive of knowledge and discernment. But we will not gladly forego present delights if we do not yet fully taste the sweetness of God with all our sense.[19]

This is not a world-denying doctrine, but rather an affirmation of that to which the whole world points. Nothing is evil by nature, because God only creates what is good. The tendency to evil, the habit of the self-centered passions, is no match for the goodness of nature. In this, Diadochus is consciously opposing the doctrines of the Messalians, who had a more dualistic idea of the substantiality of evil. For them, life was a constant struggle between good and evil as forces on the same battlefield. Victory was only possible through constant prayer in the Spirit by those called "the perfect," who had risen beyond the mundane pleasures of this life. With Diadochus you get the sense that he is somewhat of a reluctant ascetic. He enjoys his food, he savors his wine, and he only fasts because he has found a better form of sustenance, a sense of taste more satisfying than the physical body can afford. He fasts because it enables him to feast more completely, to reach satiety of the love of God, and be content. But this is, after all, the common practice of Orthodoxy: times of fasting and feasting are purposely alternated to allow the full meaning of the church's year to be enacted physically as well as spiritually. Fasting and prayer are the two wings of the ascetical life: they enable the Christian to celebrate and feast appropriately as the seasons turn, and as the festivals of saints prepare the faithful for the banquet of heaven. Sometimes believers are even forbidden to fast, if the season is a joyful celebration, or if the beginning of the time of fasting requires a clear beginning and end, lest the one who fasts draws attention to him- or herself leading to pride.

> Just as a body overburdened by the abundance of foods causes the mind to become sluggish and lazy, so too when weakened from exaggerated vigilance it brings about a certain melancholy as well as repugnance for the Word in the contemplative part of the soul. Therefore, one has to prepare foods for oneself according to the movements of the body so that when it is healthy it may be aptly kept in check. When it is weak, it should be moderately fattened. A warrior should not fatigue himself bodily but should have what he needs that he might do battle so that through bodily labours he will be sufficiently purified.[20]

All things in moderation—that is the message here. Trying to strain the ascetic practices can only lead to an unnecessary tension, a melancholy like that produced by the *akedia* described by Evagrius as one of the Eight Thoughts. Not many of the desert fathers and mothers counsel that the body should be "moderately fattened" if it has become too weak. Every good gift comes from God, and should be received with thanks. All of this exhibits a mother's care for her child:

> God is like a mother who momentarily refuses to carry in her arms her little one who is unruly with regard to nursing so that, thus frightened by the foul-looking men and the beasts that surround him, he goes back to his mother's lap in tears and great fear . . . But we are not children of desertion—far from it!—but we believe ourselves to be legitimate children of God's grace, and we are nursed by it through little desolations and rich consolations, so that, in his goodness, we might urge ourselves on to become perfect in the fullness of maturity.[21]

God is patient with us as a mother is with her nursing child. Sometimes a little discipline is needed to keep the child safe, so that they learn whom to trust and whom to fear. But God never deserts his children, any more than a mother could abandon a child. "As a mother comforts her child, so I will comfort you; you shall be comforted in Jerusalem" (Isa 66:13).

But still, restorative rations are not an end in themselves; they are necessary to build up one's strength ready for the recommencement of the battle. Chief among the weapons of the spiritual war is the recitation of the holy Name:

> The intellect demands us back absolutely whenever we block up all its exits by the recollection of God—which is the work which ought fully to occupy its industry. So one must give it the 'Lord Jesus' [*kyrie iesou*] alone for a perfect undertaking of this end; for it says, 'no one says "Lord Jesus" except in the holy Spirit' [1 Cor. 12.3]. Let one constantly contemplate this phrase carefully in his own treasuries in this way, lest he turn aside into any fantasies. As many as attend to this holy and glorious name ceaselessly in the depth of their heart are always able to see the light of their intellect—since governed by reason with a strict solicitude, it burns up the sordidness which prevails in the soul, with a strong sensation; for it also says, 'Our God is a consuming fire' [Heb. 12.29].[22]

Here we again have one of the earliest examples of the use of a short form of prayer that can be seen as an alternative to the longer forms of liturgical prayer such as the Lord's Prayer or the "Hail, Mary." We have already seen how Macarius the Great recommended a form of monologistic prayer, a short exclamation or cry to God when in trouble, or as a simple entrusting of oneself to the all-embracing mercy of God. Here Diadochus recommends the constant repetition of the divine Name as a discipline of the mind, to stop the attention from being distracted by other things. He interprets St. Paul's letter to the Corinthians as an exhortation to the recitation of the name of the Lord as a repeated cry of distress from a troubled soul, or as a response of a heart bathed in the light of the intellect, a light not originating from itself but emerging from the very heart of God, a light in which the soul desires to be bathed. It is not so much that the Spirit enables us to make the creedal confession that "Jesus is Lord"; rather, we are enabled to cry out that name of the Lord Jesus, whether in desperation, as a drowning sailor pleading for help, or in delight, as a swimmer completely at ease in a warm Mediterranean Sea.

Such a practice comes with "a strong sensation," a burning like that of an iron being thrust into the oven of a blacksmith's forge before emerging radiant with heat, pliant for the job at hand. This is not a matter of gentle restoration by the application of a mild paint-stripper, this is the lighting of a blowtorch to burn off all impurities, revealing the hidden strength and beauty of the iron of the soul.

But it is God who is the cosmic blacksmith, with scars on his hands and arms, and sweat dripping from his brow from exposure to the heat. The remembrance of the Lord Jesus is not achieved by our own strength, but by the grace of God going before us, "preventing" us in the language of the collects of Thomas Cranmer:

> When the soul is agitated by anger, or blurry-eyed from a hangover, or discouraged by onerous worries, even if it should forcefully strain itself, the mind cannot attain the memory of the Lord Jesus Christ on its own. Thus darkened by its restless passions, the mind becomes a stranger to its own sense. And so the vehemence of the passions entrenches the memory in callousness, the soul's desire finds nowhere to set its seal that the mind might bear the mark of meditation. Nevertheless, if the soul is freed of the passions, even though, through forgetfulness, the longed-for object is briefly stolen away, the mind can quickly resume its normal activity and fervently reclaim its longed-for saving treasure.
>
> Then the soul can meditate on this grace and thereby proclaim with it, 'Lord Jesus,' just as a mother might teach her son to say 'daddy,' repeating along with him until she brings him to say it clearly—even in his sleep—and he no longer makes meaningless noises. That is why the Apostle says, in the same way, the Spirit too comes to help us in our weakness; for we do not know how

> to pray as we ought, but the Spirit itself intercedes with inexpressible groans [Rom. 8.26].[23]

It is not often that one can find in this type of literature a cure for a hangover! But Diadochus freely admits that "the spirit indeed is willing, but the flesh is weak" (Matt 26:41). The passions are restless and vehement, making the soul callous and a blunt weapon in the hand of the spiritual warrior. And yet there is always hope. It is grace that is needed to complete this work, the self-effacing grace of a mother guiding her child to faith in the paternal love of God. Nonetheless it is hard work training the mind to always resort to the grace that is eternally offered and can be continuously received by making the mind open and expansive. It is a hidden work, a secret rejoicing that is best kept unobserved by others who would not understand the mysteries of this new birth.

To speak too freely of such experiences is to undermine their effectiveness:

> As when the doors of the baths are left open it causes the heat to escape from inside, so too, when a soul wants to speak much, even though all that she has to say is good, she dissipates the memory through the door of the voice. Thus deprived of opportune thoughts a soul unloads her indiscreet considerations on the first person she runs in to, because she no longer has the Holy Spirit who protects her thoughts from fantasy.[24]

Having warned the reader not to overdo their regime of fasting, and given advice to those who have overindulged in wine, Diadochus draws an image from the public baths, the saunas of the ancient world. "Can you close the door, please?" he imagines someone saying after an inconsiderate fellow patron leaves the door swinging on its hinges. And the spiritual life is indeed a kind of hothouse, a sweat lodge for the incubation of visions. To work properly there needs to be a kind of benign greenhouse effect, an effort not to dissipate the energy concentrated by one's prayers. In this case the door to be closed is the voice, or rather the mouth itself, keeping the heat within.

And yet what better way to use one's time in the bath or shower than to sing?

> When the soul enjoys the fulness of its innate fruits, she sings the Psalms with more strength and prefers to pray with a louder voice. But when she is moved by the Holy Spirit, she chants and prays in the solitude of her own heart with all abandon and sweetness . . .
>
> When we are burdened by heavy discouragement we should raise our voices a bit more in psalmody, making the sounds of the soul harmonize with hope's joy unto such point that the dark clouds are driven away by the breath of song.[25]

"The one who sings prays twice," says Augustine of Hippo, famously, in his commentary on the Psalms. The Psalter was the hymn book of the early church, and of course of Judaism before that. Perpetual recitation of the psalms was the chief aid to the constant recollection of God. This is the true cleansing of the body and soul—heartfelt repentance, thanksgiving for gifts received, and offering oneself to God in devotion and praise.

> Whoever intends his heart to be cleansed, let him set it on fire by the recollection of the Lord at all times, having this alone as his concern and unceasing work. For those who decide to cast off their own rottenness must not sometimes pray and sometimes not; rather one must always devote oneself to prayer in guarding the intellect, even if one dwells outside the houses of prayer. Because in this way one who intends to purify gold, if he permits the fire of the smelting furnace to ease off even for a short period, he makes the matter being purified hard again; so also for someone who recollects God sometimes but sometimes not; that which he seems to gain through prayer, he loses through taking time off. It is characteristic of a man who loves virtue always to consume the earthiness of the heart in the recollection of God, so that as the bad is consumed little by little by the fire of the recollection of the good, the soul might return to its natural brightness perfectly, with additional glory.[26]

Questions for reflection and discussion

- Do you ever use "monologistic" (single word) prayer? What benefit does it bring?
- Have you ever belonged to a community of people who pray together?
- Which is more important in prayer—the body or the soul? Why?

Further reading

Tim Vivian, 2004, *Saint Macarius the Spiritbearer: Coptic Texts Relating to Saint Macarius the Great*, New York: St Vladimir's Seminary Press.

George A. Maloney SJ, 1992, *Pseudo-Macarius: The Fifty Spiritual Homilies and the Great Letter*, Classics of Western Spirituality, New York: Paulist Press.

Cliff Ermatinger, 2010, *Following the Footsteps of the Invisible: The Complete Works of Diadochus of Photikē*, Collegeville, MN: Liturgical Press.

Notes

1 George A. Maloney SJ, 1992, *Pseudo-Macarius: The Fifty Spiritual Homilies and the Great Letter*, Classics of Western Spirituality, New York: Paulist Press, p. 37.

2 Tim Vivian, 2004, *Saint Macarius the Spiritbearer: Coptic Texts Relating to Saint Macarius the Great*, New York: St Vladimir's Seminary Press, p. 104.

3 *Praktikos* 29; John Eudes Bamberger OCSO, 1981, *Evagrius Ponticus: The Praktikos & Chapters on Prayer*, Collegeville, MN: Cistercian Publications, p. 24.

4 Benedicta Ward SLG, 1975/1984 revd edn, *The Sayings of the Desert Fathers: The Alphabetical Collection*, Collegeville, MN: Cistercian Publications, p. 131.

5 Vivian, *Macarius*, p. 76.

6 Quoted by Kallistos Ware in Maloney, *Pseudo-Macarius*, p. xi.

7 Maloney, *Pseudo-Macarius*, pp. 76–7.

8 Maloney, *Pseudo-Macarius*, p. 87.

9 Maloney, *Pseudo-Macarius*, p. 47.

10 Maloney, *Pseudo-Macarius*, p. 47.

11 Maloney, *Pseudo-Macarius*, p. 81.

12 Maloney, *Pseudo-Macarius*, pp. 81, 82.

13 Maloney, *Pseudo-Macarius*, p. 83.

14 Maloney, *Pseudo-Macarius*, p. 145.

15 Andrew Louth, 1981, *The Origins of the Christian Mystical Tradition: From Plato to Denys*, Oxford: Clarendon Press, pp. 130–1.

16 Janet Elaine Rutherford, 2000, *One Hundred Practical Texts of Perception and Spiritual Discernment from Diadochos of Photike*, Belfast Byzantine Texts and Translations, 8, Belfast: Byzantine Enterprises, p. 25.

17 Rutherford, *Diadochos*, pp. 25–7.

18 Rutherford, *Diadochos*, p. 55.

19 Cliff Ermatinger, 2010, *Following the Footsteps of the Invisible: The Complete Works of Diaodochus of Photikē*, Collegeville, MN: Liturgical Press, p. 89.

20 Ermatinger, *Following the Footsteps*, p. 89.

21 Ermatinger, *Following the Footsteps*, pp. 115–16.

22 Rutherford, *Diadochos*, pp. 73–5.

23 Ermatinger, *Following the Footsteps*, pp. 95–6.

24 Ermatinger, *Following the Footsteps*, pp. 102–3.

25 Ermatinger, *Following the Footsteps*, pp. 104–5.

26 Rutherford, *Diadochos*, pp. 147–9.

4

Mark the Ascetic, John Climacus and the Ascent of Mount Sinai

Sometime during the 380s CE, a devout Christian woman by the name of Egeria made a pilgrimage to Egypt and the Holy Land, keeping a journal of her discoveries as she went. Her book provides a detailed description of the places she visited and the liturgical practices of the churches in which she worshipped. Her travelogue is a mine of information, although she does have a tendency to end a section by saying "and the rest they do in the usual way," which is precisely the information that we no longer have and would dearly like to know. On her itinerary was the holy mountain of Sinai, and this is where she begins her account:

> We were walking along between the mountains, and came to a spot where they opened out to form an endless valley—a huge plain, and very beautiful—across which we could see Sinai, the holy Mount of God. Next to the spot where the mountains open out is the place of the 'Graves of Craving' [where the Israelites were buried who had craved for the plenty of Egypt (Num. 11.34)]. When we arrived there our guides, the holy men who were with us, said, 'It is usual for the people who come here to say a prayer when first they catch sight of the Mount of God' and we did as they suggested. The Mount of God is perhaps four miles away from where we were, right across the huge valley I have mentioned . . . This is the huge flat valley in which the children of Israel were waiting while holy Moses went up into the Mount of God and was there 'forty days and forty nights' . . . It was at the head of this very valley that holy Moses pastured the cattle of his father-in-law and God spoke to him twice from the burning bush.[1]

The famous monastery of St Catherine at the base of Mount Sinai was yet to be built, being constructed between 548 and 565 by the Byzantine emperor Justinian I. It is the world's oldest continuously inhabited Christian monastery, a site protected by both Christian and Muslim leaders through the centuries. The most famous of the abbots in charge of the monastery is known to us by the name of John Climacus (c. 579–649), or "John of the Ladder," after the book he wrote entitled *The Ladder of Divine Ascent*. This book is traditionally read aloud in Orthodox monastic refectories every year during the Great Fast of Lent, for the edification of the monks and nuns. The laity too have often turned to this book as a guide to the spiritual life, with John insisting that marriage is not an obstacle to holiness, even if he himself is writing specifically with monks in mind. The way is open to all as long as they have an experienced guide and companions on the way.

The Ladder has 30 steps (the years of the hidden life of Christ until his baptism), beginning with renunciation and detachment; climbing through the vices and virtues such as hatred and malice, simplicity and humility; leading finally to union with God in stillness, prayer, dispassion and love. John writes in his first chapter of the universality of the call of God:

> God is the life of all free beings. He is the salvation of all, of believers or unbelievers, of the just or the unjust, of the pious or the impious, of those freed from passions or caught up in them, of monks or those living in the world, of the educated or the illiterate, of the healthy or the sick, of the young or the very old. He is like the outpouring of light, the glimpse of the sun, or the changes of the weather, which are the same for everyone without exception.[2]

As St. Paul says in his speech to the Athenians at the Areopagus: "God . . . is not far from each one of us. 'For in him we live and move and have our being' " (Acts 17:27-28). Or as the Qur'an says: "God is closer to us than our jugular vein" (Surah Qaf, 16). In the quotation above, John Climacus is probably thinking of the Sermon on the Mount where Jesus tells his disciples to love their enemies, "so that you may be children of your Father in heaven; for he makes his sun rise on the evil and on the good, and sends rain on the righteous and on the unrighteous" (Matt 5:45). To do good to others, even those who persecute you, to the best of your ability, is a fundamental teaching of John's *Ladder*. It is a matter of returning to our created nature as fundamentally good rather than intrinsically evil. Friendship with God is the most natural thing in the world. God has made us to be God's friends; we are children of love, and it is self-control that enables us to feel the warmth of that love kindled within us. It is not a simple exercise, but it promises great rewards:

> Let all those coming to this marvellous, tough and painful—though also easy—contest leap, as it were, into a fire, so that a non-material flame may take up residence within them . . . At the beginning of our religious life, we cultivate the virtues, and we do so with toil and difficulty. Progressing a little, we then lose our sense of grief or retain very little of it. But when our mortal intelligence turns to zeal and is mastered by it, then we work with full joy, determination, desire, and a holy flame.[3]

This is not a cold disdain for the things of this world, but a scorching flame of desire for God, a determination to invest all of one's energies in this work of purification. The "sense of grief," alluded to by John, is the gift of tears as an expression of lamentation for the years not well spent, the repentance known in Greek as *penthos* (*πένθος*). It is the godly sorrow that can especially characterize the early years of earnestly living a spiritual life, a wish that one had found this way sooner and had been less desultory in one's prayer and in service of others. For many, tears can be a continuing experience of conversion: tears shed for oneself as layer after layer of resistance to grace is unearthed; and tears shed for others, sharing in the tears of Jesus as he weeps over Jerusalem (see Luke 19:41-42). Tears can also be an expression of joy, in gratitude for the gift of God's felt presence even amid personal weakness, and in thanksgiving for prayers answered.

Living alone together

In Step 1 of *The Ladder*, John describes the basic forms of monastic living:

> All monastic life may be said to take one of three forms. There is the road of withdrawal and solitude for the spiritual athlete; there is the life of stillness [*hesychia*] shared with one or two others; there is the practice of living patiently in community.[4]

John himself had experienced all three of these types of religious life, from the age of 16 when he first entered the monastery. For the first three years John was guided by the elder monk Abba Martyrius, who appears to have died shortly after he had tonsured John as a monk. Thereafter, John lived as a hermit for the next 40 years, only coming down to live in community when he was elected as abbot. Of the three ways of living the monastic life listed above, his recommendation to others was to follow the second type, "the life of stillness shared with one or two others," as he believed it provided the most benefit from both a deepened silence and a shared solitude. Here again is the value of *hesychia*, of stillness at the heart of activity, and silence out of which appropriate speech can emerge. Silence is a great help in the discipline of attentiveness to the "still, small voice of God" or "a sound of sheer silence" (1 Kings 19:12), as heard by Elijah in the solitude of Mount Horeb.

Although Elijah is the archetypal hermit, journeying out to the wilderness and being fed miraculously by the ravens, still there is a natural and divine momentum to share the benefits of silence with others. Solitude, as so many solitaries have found, is a way to realize the interconnectedness of us all. Just sharing the spiritual life with others is a help along the way, a natural way of life that answers some of the needs God saw in his son Adam, realizing that "It is not good that the man should be alone; I will make him a helper as his partner" (Gen 2:18). In the second Genesis account of the creation of humanity God offers the animal kingdom to Adam, for him to name them and to realize his connection with them all. But it is only with another person that Adam discovers who he is in partnership, a companionship celebrated in marriage or in committed celibate community. As the psalmist says: "How very good and pleasant it is when kindred live together in unity!" (Ps 133:1). John Climacus realized from his own experience some of the pitfalls of a solitary life, bringing out one of his typically lively images:

> Community life is opposed to despondency. But she is a constant companion of the hermit. She will never leave him till his death, and wrestles with him daily till his end. Seeing an anchorite's cell, she smiles, and creeps up and camps nearby. A doctor visits the sick in the morning, but despondency visits ascetics about noonday.[5]

Despondency, the "noonday demon" (see Ps 91:6), is no stranger to the monk or nun, especially the one who lives alone. They see her on her rounds at midday when the sun is hottest and it's still three hours till the daily meal. The religious life lived with others ideally offers the freedom of a measured solitude, while maintaining the mutual support necessary to sustain the vocation of one troubled (as many are) by the temptation of despair. We have already seen how Evagrius has a keen eye for the inner narratives of despondency, and John adds his own comments to continue the diagnosis of this spiritual disease, prescribing fire, fervor, zeal and love, as he rounds off the description of the first rung on the ladder that reaches to heaven:

> So who is a faithful and wise monk? He who has kept his fervour unabated, and to the end of his life has not ceased daily to add fire to fire, fervour to fervour, zeal to zeal, love to love. This is the first step. Let him who has set foot on it not turn back.[6]

Climbing the Ladder of Divine Ascent is not a day-long excursion for casual tourists, but a life-long discipline to be learned and practiced day after day. It requires all the energy and courage one can muster in order to become at all proficient in this skill: fervor and zeal are cast into the fire of love, allowing the dross that rises to the surface to be discarded, and the molten metal of compassion to pour as liquid rock from the flaming coals.

A deviser of seasonings

John, like his precursor Evagrius, is keenly aware of each of the thoughts, the "passions" that plague the mind of one seeking stillness. First on the list of Evagrius, and halfway through the itinerary of John, we find the struggle with gluttony:

> Gluttony is hypocrisy of the stomach; for when it is glutted it complains of scarcity, and when it is loaded and bursting it cries out that it is hungry. Gluttony is a deviser of seasonings, a source of sweet dishes. You stop one jet and it bobs up elsewhere; you plug this too, and you open another. Gluttony is a delusion of the eyes which receives in moderation but wants to gobble everything at once.[7]

There is an expression not heard so much recently: "My eyes were bigger than my stomach," spoken apologetically by an embarrassed guest with half a steak pie remaining on their plate. Gluttony can sometimes be a matter of etiquette, with an accompanying virtue of not wanting to be critical of an overly generous host. It takes some sensitivity to decline without giving offence. John himself sees the funny side of this failing, picturing the demon of gluttony as "a deviser of seasonings," like an ambitious contestant on a TV cooking competition, pouring all the spices they can find into a bubbling, steaming pot. Is it a mischievous glint in the corner of their eye, or just a drop of salty sweat that further serves to season the dish? Gluttony, according to John, is a delusion of the eyes not of the stomach, a failure of perception of what is enough and what is too much. Moderation is the only antidote, and that is produced in the mind, not found in the refrigerator.

In all these struggles God does not require perfection, only a willingness to try:

> Constantly wrestle with your thought, and whenever it wanders call it back to you. God does not require from those still under obedience prayer completely free of distractions. Do not despair

> when your thoughts are filched, but remain calm and unceasingly recall your mind. Unbroken recollection is proper only to an angel.[8]

"What should I do if I am distracted a hundred times in my half hour of silent prayer?" says the eager but frustrated disciple. "You should say to yourself," says the wise old monastic (in this case the Cistercian Thomas Keating), "How wonderful! A hundred opportunities to return to the Lord in prayer!"

If gluttony tends to come early in the lists of the afflictive passions that steal our thoughts away, the demons of vainglory and pride tend to hide away till the last possible minute. Even a certain self-control of the thoughts can itself be the immediate precursor to pride.

> The sun shines on all alike, and vainglory beams on all activities. For instance, I am vainglorious when I fast, and when I relax the fast in order to be unnoticed I am again vainglorious over my prudence. When well-dressed I am quite overcome by vainglory, and when I put on poor clothes I am vainglorious again. When I talk I am defeated, and when I am silent I am again defeated.[9]

Sometimes you just can't win! Do I have that extra helping of apple pie, or do I leave it on the plate, making a display of frugality while knowing that the leftover portion is likely to be thrown away? Do I browse for clothes at a charity shop and so cultivate an image of trend-setting "poverty," or buy from the cheapest sweatshop retailer and exploit their labor, or go for a named brand because they last longer? There's no way of avoiding some kind of moral dilemma. Even monks can be proud of the number of patches on their habit, or their pair of spectacles held together by a strip of tape.

Sometimes these debates involve more than one voice at a time:

> One who had the gift of sight told me what he had seen. 'Once,' he said, 'when I was sitting in assembly, the demon of vainglory and the demon of pride came and sat beside me, one on either side. The one poked me in the side with the finger of vainglory and urged me to relate some vision or labour which I had done

> in the desert. But as soon as I had shaken him off, saying: 'Let them be turned back and put to shame who plot evil against me' [Ps. 40.14], then the demon on my left at once said in my ear: 'Well done, well done, you have become great . . . ' Turning to him, I made apt use of the rest of the verse and said: 'Let them be turned back and put to shame who said to me: "Well done, well done."'[10]

Mark the Ascetic and the sequence of seduction

Sometime in the early fifth century, a man known simply as Mark the Monk, or Mark the Ascetic, became a hermit in the deserts of either Egypt or Palestine. Mark was one of the founders of the hesychastic movement in Eastern Christianity, practicing prayer in the ways of stillness or silence (*ἡσυχία/hesychia*), as he writes in his treatise *On Those who Think that They are Made Righteous by Works* 29–31:

> Stillness helps us by making evil inoperative . . . It is the most direct support in attaining dispassion. The intellect cannot be still unless the body is still also; and the wall between them cannot be demolished without stillness and prayer.[11]

For Mark, as for Evagrius before him, dispassion (*ἀπάθεια/apatheia*) is of great importance in the contemplative life. It is only when the heart is sufficiently still that the intellect can have clear enough vision to see what is going on. Mark commends stillness of the body, remarking on the interdependency of body and mind. Both are saved together, or not at all. Much of the wisdom of the hesychasts was learned in the patient observance of how the body and its senses affect the mind. It is only personal experience surveyed with an almost scientific analysis that enables the individual to learn, for better or for worse, the intertwining of sensations, feelings and thoughts.

The discernment of the thoughts and their causes is crucial to the ability to overcome them before they become afflictive passions.

It is not a matter of trying to blank out the mind but of seeing clearly what is going on. Personal experience and alert understanding of causation is necessary for a lasting freedom to be found. The sequence of moral causation is explained by Mark as he describes the process of temptation (*πειρασμός/peirasmos*), writing in his treatise *On the Spiritual Law* (138–142):

> When we have freed ourselves from every voluntary sin of the mind, we should then fight against the passions which result from prepossession [*πρόληψις/prolepsis*].
>
> Prepossession is the involuntary presence of former sins in the memory. At the stage of active warfare we try to prevent it from developing into a passion [*πάθος/pathos*]; after victory it is repulsed while still but a provocation.
>
> A provocation [*προσβολή/prosbole*] is an image-free stimulation in the heart. Like a mountain-pass, the experienced take control of it ahead of the enemy.
>
> Once our thoughts are accompanied by images we have already given them our assent [*συγκατάθεσις/sunkatathesis*]; for a provocation does not involve us in guilt so long as it is not accompanied by images.[12]

This is quite a dense paragraph of ascetic theology, but one that has proved very helpful to those who continue to struggle with their thoughts, even after they have gained some experience of how the thoughts affect the soul. We have already been discussing some of the sins that voluntarily obsess the mind; here we begin to uncover the involuntary, even unconscious, processes that allow these kinds of thoughts to take control of our lives. Although Mark does not describe the process of temptation from beginning to end, one step after the other, there is a clear linear sequence that emerges: provocation → assent → prepossession → passion. Largely working backwards, tracing the passions to their roots, Mark is able to see how patterns of thought take on a life of their own, gradually insinuating themselves into the habitual mind-states, known in this tradition as the passions. Provocation is the first stirring of the process, still image-free, the provocation coming from the demons rather than oneself, though as Mark warns at the end of the passage, the monk or nun may put themselves in the way of trouble by not avoiding the causes of the initial assault. But then, sooner or later, the mind clothes the impressions with images, memories, or fantasies and gives assent to the thoughts. This leads to a "prepossession," a habit-energy or predisposition to sin that all too easily leads to the full-blown state of addictive passion.

Images in the mind are incredibly powerful. These days the use of active visualization in meditation is often praised as a way to the healing of body and mind. Somehow the mind's eye, our spiritual perception, magnifies the will to love and to bring healing to oneself and others. But it works the other way too. Imagining all the good things we are missing out on, or conversely picturing all the things that might teach our enemies a lesson, is not going to help us in the spiritual life. Who knows what happens to a person's mind when it is bombarded by images of all the material things that could be ours if we so desired, or the war games that rejoice in the destruction of the enemy? Sometimes the only way out is to flee, to reach for the off switch, pull out the plug and head for the garden or the woods:

> Some people flee away from these thoughts like 'a brand plucked out of the fire' (Zech. 3.2); but others dally with them, and so get burnt. Do not say: 'I don't want it, but it happens.' For even though you may not want the thing itself, yet you welcome what causes it.[13]

We may want to be chaste, in the abstract, but in actuality rather enjoy the battle; or we find ourselves fighting in the wrong battlefield altogether, not noticing the subtleties of the chain of causation. It may be that we are unsuccessfully trying to be pure in heart when the real problem is a judgemental spirit that alienates us from others and hinders the development of chaste yet affectionate friendship. We may accuse ourselves of pride, when what we need is a stronger dose of self-respect and gratitude for the gifts God has given us.

A key aspect of this description of temptation is that there is no sin in being provoked. The initial thought may become sinful if it is assented to and allowed to become first a predisposition and then a habitual state, but the initial thought is morally neutral. It is only at the higher reaches of the spiritual life that such provocations begin to fade away. Indeed, they may become worse, more distracting, as the seeker discovers more and more layers of delusion to be wiped away, as John Climacus explains:

> We should not be dismayed if we find that our passions are stronger at the beginning of our monastic life than they were in our life in the world. For we have to remove the causes of sickness, and then health will come to us. The beasts were there in hiding all the time, only they did not show themselves.[14]

But this is where the practice of stillness, of letting go of discursive thought, is so helpful in the process of learning dispassion, and we have the chance to practice the real object of the exercise which is to have a clear eye that enables the heart to love. A great aid in this practice, if not an absolute necessity, is the steadfast love and support of a spiritual guide. Revealing one's thoughts to one's mentor enables the burden of a sense of sinfulness to be shared, and through confession of sins in the Sacrament of Reconciliation, and the healing grace of Holy Communion, a new beginning is made possible. Ultimately it is Christ who invites the weary to find rest for their souls, and who gently reassures us that "I am gentle and humble in heart . . . For my yoke is easy, and my burden is light" (Matt 11:29-30).

Snakes and ladders

In his *Ladder of Divine Ascent*, John gives his own version of the process of temptation, with a slightly fuller and more polished presentation of the steps involved:

> Among the discerning Fathers, distinctions are recognized between provocations, coupling, assent, captivity, struggle, and the disease called passion, which is in the soul. These blessed fathers say that provocation is a simple word or image encountered for the first time, which has entered into the heart. Coupling is con-

> versation with what has been encountered, whether this be passionately or otherwise. Assent is the delighted yielding of the soul to what it has encountered. Captivity is a forcible and unwilling abduction of the heart, a permanent lingering with what we have encountered, and which totally undermines the necessary order of our souls. By struggle they mean force equal to that which is leading the attack, and this force wins or loses according to the desires of the spirit. Passion, in their view, is properly something that lies hidden for a long time in the soul and by its very presence it takes on the character of a habit until the soul of its own accord clings to it with affection.[15]

Like Mark the Ascetic, John reaffirms that the first link in the chain, the provocation, is by no means morally culpable. Things arise in the mind beyond our conscious control. It is only as the sequence develops that we get into trouble. In this analysis, this biopsy of the soul, John then adds the stages of "coupling" (*συνδυασμός/sunduasmos*) and "struggle" (*πάλη/pale*), though "struggle" is placed before "captivity" in the paragraph that followed, which seems a more logical place for it to be. Of these stages in the process of temptation, the first, "provocation," is free of sin. "Coupling," "assent," and "struggle" are not always sinful, depending on "the condition of the soul." Even in "captivity" there may be mitigating circumstances; but "passion" is denounced and seen as the immediate precursor to sinful action. The safest form of defense is to cut off the sequence after the first encounter, to eradicate the chain of thought at its very inception. So it would seem that in John Climacus we have the sequence: provocation → coupling → assent → [struggle →] captivity → passion.

There is just one further refinement to the description of temptation, where Climacus picks up a suggestion from the writings of Mark the Ascetic:

> Amongst the more precise and discerning Fathers there is mention of a still more subtle notion, something which some of them call a flick of the mind (*παραρριπισμός/pararripismos)*. This is its characteristic: without passage of time, without a word or image,

> it instantaneously introduces the passion to the victim. There is nothing swifter than this in the material world or more indiscernible in the spiritual. It manifests itself in the soul by a simple remembrance, with which the soul has no time to dally, since it is independent of time, unconnected with any image, impervious to analysis, and in some cases even unknown to the person himself.[16]

It is perhaps best to view this as a momentary reflex of the mind that can happen at any time, pointing to the alert vigilance needed on behalf of the one who prays, so as to recognize such thoughts in an instant and return to the state of dispassionate calm.

Hesychia

In all of this, John, like Mark before him, praises the virtue of stillness (*hesychia*), both of body and soul:

> Stillness of the body is the accurate knowledge and management of one's feelings and perceptions. Stillness of soul is the accurate knowledge of one's thoughts and is an unassailable mind. Brave and determined thinking is a friend of stillness. It is always on the watch at the doors of the heart, killing or driving off invading notions. What I mean by this will be well understood by the one who practices stillness in the deep places of the heart, while the novice will have no experience or knowledge of it. A shrewd hesychast requires no words. They are enlightened by deeds rather than by words.[17]

Of key importance here is the stress on direct personal experience. John does not want his disciples to be armchair ascetics, reading books on prayer rather than committing time to prayer itself. Not that there is anything wrong in study—he was an educated, eloquent man himself—but to get the full benefit of his teaching you had to know to your bones the secrets of watchfulness. Deeds not words are needed here. Then if the certainty of personal experience is laid as a secure foundation it doesn't matter where you practice your life of prayer: noisy, or quiet, all places and all bodies are temples of the Holy Spirit:

> The start of stillness is the rejection of all noisiness as something that will trouble the depths of the soul. The final point is when one has no longer a fear of noisy disturbance, when one is immune to it . . . Strange as it may seem, the hesychast is one who fights to keep their incorporeal self shut up in the house of the body.[18]

And the body is with you wherever you go. It is the desert itself, a cave in the rock, a hermitage at the top of Mount Sinai where Moses met with God, heard his words, and was transfigured by the light of eternity:

> The one who has achieved stillness has arrived at the very centre of the mysteries . . . Paul confirms this. If he had not been caught up into Paradise as into stillness, he would never have heard the unspeakable words (cf. 2 Cor. 12.3, 4).[19]

Stillness is the place of revelation, the uncarved stone on which the words of God are engraved, the seasoned hewn wood on which the icon of Christ is written, the unresisting dust in which Jesus writes of mercy not of judgement, with his uncondemning hand. Being caught up into paradise like St. Paul, wordless and without a sound, is the preparation for the sound of sheer silence to be heard, the oxygen of the breath of God to fill our aching lungs.

Stillness and the Jesus Prayer

> Stillness is worshipping God unceasingly and waiting on Him. Let the remembrance of Jesus be present with your every breath. Then indeed you will appreciate the value of stillness.[20]

Here we have in the writings of John Climacus what may be a very early reference to the Jesus Prayer, "Lord Jesus Christ, Son of God, have mercy on me!" We have seen in an earlier chapter how

Diadochus recommends the recitation of the name "Lord Jesus." In this passage from John the full sentence of the Prayer is not quoted, so it may be a simple invocation of the Person of Christ rather than a particular phrase, or just the name "Jesus" itself, that is repeated. The exhortation may simply be to pray continuously, or taken literally as a recitation of the Prayer or the Name following the rhythm of the breath. Whatever the exact teaching here, continuity of prayer in all circumstances is clearly encouraged.

In another place John has a similar teaching: "Let the remembrance of death and the concise Jesus Prayer go to sleep with you and get up with you, for nothing helps you as these do when you are asleep."[21] The phrase "concise Jesus Prayer" is translated elsewhere as "the Prayer of Jesus said as a monologue."[22] It may be that the "Jesus Prayer" referred to here is the "Our Father," the Lord's Prayer, but later hesychasts, such as Gregory Palamas in his *Triads*, clearly interpreted "the remembrance of Jesus," and "the Prayer of Jesus," as referring to the full invocation of the Jesus Prayer itself. In any case, it is a quality of attentiveness to the presence of God in Christ, aware of the fragility of life and the inescapable final judgement, that carries the believer through the night until the dawn.

Perhaps it is good that the earliest references to the Jesus Prayer seem to allow a variety of forms, as this can legitimize praying the Prayer in various ways today. The Prayer can be longer or shorter, depending on how it is most easily and effectively implanted in the heart. The longest form in common use is the phrase: "Lord Jesus Christ, Son of the Living God, have mercy on me, a sinner!" This form clearly shows the biblical roots of the Jesus Prayer, beginning with Peter's confession to Jesus that, "You are the Christ, the Son of the living God!" (Matt 16:16), and the cry of blind Bartimeus outside the gates of Jericho as Jesus walked by: "Jesus, Son of David, have mercy on me!" (Mark 10:47); and combining this with the prayer of the publican in the temple, "God, be merciful to me, a sinner!" (Luke 18:13). In the Greek tradition of saying the Jesus Prayer, the epithet "a sinner" is not often used; and some teachers allow for the substitution of the word "us" for "me." The two irreducible poles of the prayer are the Name of Jesus, and the exhortation to "have mercy." Even here, all can sometimes be reduced to the simple exclamation "Jesus." In Greek the name is pronounced "*Iesous*" (*Ἰησοῦς*), or "*Iesou*" (*Ἰησοῦ*) in the vocative form, the form by which one cries out to another to attract their attention. The name is a transliteration of the Hebrew "*Yeshua*," meaning "God saves," and so is itself both a cry for help and a reassurance of the help that will surely come.

Probably the earliest example of the Jesus Prayer as we know it today comes from a record of the teaching of Abba Philimon in Egypt in the sixth or seventh century, roughly contemporary with John Climacus. A brother is described as coming to Abba Philimon in despair, complaining that his thoughts travel everywhere and he finds no joy in the practice of prayer. Philimon replies that he feels this way because he has not realized the warmth of the longing for God:

> The brother said to him: 'What shall I do, father?' Abba Philimon replied: 'Meditate inwardly for a while, deep in your heart; for this can cleanse your intellect of these things.' The brother, not understanding what was said, asked the Elder: 'What is inward meditation, father?' The Elder replied: 'Keep watch in your heart; and with watchfulness say in your mind with awe and trembling: "Lord Jesus Christ, have mercy upon me." For this is the advice which the blessed Diadochos gave to beginners.'[23]

Philimon has here interpreted the saying of Diadochus to refer to the full sentence of the Jesus Prayer, though a strict reading of the text by Diadochus implies that a shorter phrase is recommended ("Lord Jesus"), which suggests that the tradition is still evolving at that point in history. Nonetheless, Philimon is quite clear in his advice:

> This is what you should always be doing in your heart: whether eating or drinking, in company or outside your cell, or on a journey, repeat that prayer with a watchful mind and an undeflected intellect; also chant, and meditate on prayers and psalms. Even when carrying out needful tasks, do not let your intellect be idle but keep it meditating inwardly and praying. For in this way you can grasp the depths of divine Scripture and the power hidden in it, and give unceasing work to the intellect, thus fulfilling the

> apostolic command: 'Pray without ceasing' (1 Thess. 5.17). Pay strict attention to your heart and watch over it, so that it does not give admittance to thoughts that are evil or in any way vain and useless. Without interruption, whether asleep or awake, eating, drinking, or in company, let your heart inwardly and mentally at times be meditating on the psalms, at other times be repeating the prayer, 'Lord Jesus Christ, Son of God, have mercy upon me.' And when you chant, make sure that your mouth is not saying one thing while your mind is thinking about another.[24]

Here we have the fundamental exhortation and explanation of how to "pray without ceasing," as recommended by St. Philimon in response to the admonition of St. Paul. Meditate on prayers and the Scriptures by all means, but keep the Psalms and especially the Jesus Prayer as a constant background, like the wordless musical drone known as the "*ison*" sung by "*isokratae*," literally "those who hold the same note." This is used even today by Orthodox congregations singing Byzantine chant. So the undertone holds all in a harmonious key, praying to the Lord Jesus for mercy, inwardly meditating on him, and breathing the compassion of God at all times.

The benefits of passion

In explaining this dispassionate passion, John Climacus uses the analogy of a man longing for his beloved in the silent hours of the night, whispering her name, and reaching out to her in spirit with desire. In the same way, John encourages the spiritual seeker to have a passion for God:

> Someone truly in love keeps before his mind's eye the face of the beloved and embraces it there tenderly. Even during sleep the longing continues unappeased, and he murmurs to his beloved. This is how it is for the body. And that is how it is for the spirit. A man wounded by love had this to say about himself—and it really amazes me—'I sleep (because nature commands this) but my heart is awake (because of the abundance of my love)' (Song of Songs 5.2).[25]

At the end, John delights in the message of the scriptural love-poem the Song of Songs, and reveals behind the veil of foolishness the boundless wisdom of love: "I have known hesychasts whose flaming urge for God was limitless. They generated fire by fire, love by love, desire by desire."[26] The Greek word for love used in this passage is *eros* (*ἔρως*), the desire of lovers. Paradoxically, dispassion is described as the truly erotic love. Here all is worship and song, love and kindness, resting in the arms of the beloved and breathing quietly the prayer of God's mercy, the adoration of God's name.

And what does this lead to? What is the goal to which all things point? John Climacus sums up all his teaching in the simple word, "love."

> And now, finally, after all that we have said, there remain these three that bind and secure the union of all, faith, hope, and love; and the greatest of these is love, for God himself is so called . . . Love, by reason of its nature, is a resemblance to God, as far as that is possible for mortals; in its activity it is inebriation of the soul; and by its distinctive property it is a fountain of faith, an abyss of patience, a sea of humility.[27]

Questions for reflection and discussion

- Do you recognize the patterns of temptation outlined by Mark the Ascetic?
- How important is solitude in prayer?
- Is the journey into God an ascent or a descent? Why?

Further reading

Colm Luibheid and Norman Russell, 1982, *John Climacus: The Ladder of Divine Ascent*, Classics of Western Spirituality, New York: Paulist Press.

John Chryssavgis, 2004, *John Climacus: From the Egyptian Desert to the Sinaite Mountain*, Aldershot: Ashgate.

———, 2004, *Light Through Darkness: The Orthodox Tradition*, Traditions of Christian Spirituality Series, London: Darton, Longman & Todd.

Notes

1 John Wilkinson, 1971, *Egeria's Travels*, London: SPCK, p. 91.

2 Colm Luibheid and Norman Russell, 1982, *John Climacus: The Ladder of Divine Ascent*, Classics of Western Spirituality (CWS), New York: Paulist Press, p. 74.

3 Luibheid and Russell, *John Climacus*, pp. 76–7.

4 Luibheid and Russell, *John Climacus*, p. 79.

5 Archimandrite Lazarus Moore, 1959, *St John Climacus: The Ladder of Divine Ascent*, London: Faber and Faber, p. 138.

6 Moore, *Ascent*, p. 56.

7 Moore, *Ascent*, p. 140.

8 Moore, *Ascent*, pp. 89–90.

9 Moore, *Ascent*, p. 174.

10 Moore, *Ascent*, p. 177.

11 G. E. H. Palmer, Philip Sherrard and Kallistos Ware, 1979, 1981, 1984, 1995, 2023, *The Philokalia: The Complete Text, compiled by St Nikodimos of the Holy Mountain and St. Makarios of Corinth*, Five Volumes, Londer: Faber, vol. 1, p. 128.

12 Palmer et al, *The Philokalia*, vol. 1, pp. 119–20.

13 Palmer et al, *The Philokalia*, vol. 1, p. 120.

14 Moore, *Ascent*, p. 230.

15 Luibheid and Russell, *John Climacus*, pp. 181–2.

16 Moore, *Ascent*, p. 158.

17 Luibheid and Russell, *John Climacus*, pp. 261–2.

18 Luibheid and Russell, *John Climacus*, p. 262.

19 Luibheid and Russell, *John Climacus*, p. 264.

20 Luibheid and Russell, *John Climacus*, pp. 269–70.

21 Luibheid and Russell, *John Climacus*, p. 178.

22 Moore, *Ascent*, p. 154.

23 Palmer et al, *The Philokalia*, vol. 2, p. 347.

24 Palmer et al, *The Philokalia*, vol. 2, p. 348.

25 Luibheid and Russell, *John Climacus*, p. 287.

26 Luibheid and Russell, *John Climacus*, p. 263.

27 Moore, *Ascent*, p. 262.

5

The Two Old Men of Gaza, Hesychius of Sinai and the Art of Watchfulness

Sometime early in the sixth century, two hermit monks settled into a life of prayer and seclusion in the area of Gaza in Palestine. Barsanuphius, a Coptic Egyptian monk, came first, and was later joined by a monk called John. They were affectionately known as "the Great Old Man," and "the Other Old Man" respectively. Barsanuphius was the more renowned of the two, becoming known for the austerity of his lifestyle and the sensitivity of his counsel to those who were sick and came to him for help and healing. Around them a monastery formed, with workshops, accommodation for guests, a hospital and a church. Although many came with the express purpose of talking to the two elders, they kept strictly to their seclusion and only responded to letters requesting spiritual direction delivered by members of the community—at first the abbot Seridos, and then another monk of the community known as Dorotheus, himself a highly regarded hesychast. So strict was their solitude that at least one visitor even doubted their existence, wondering if the abbots maintained the fiction of the existence of the hermits as a ploy to increase visitors—a doubt put to rest by the Great Old Man coming down in person to wash the feet of the unbelieving traveler, before returning to his cell not having uttered a word.

The two Old Men complemented each other's ministry, sharing their responses to those seeking help. Barsanuphius inspired visitors by his words and example, while John responded more to questions of a practical, institutional nature. Both were said to have the gifts of discernment, foresight and compassion, sharing in the cure of souls, not being afraid to give frank advice even to bishops. The main aim of their letters of spiritual guidance was to encourage the downhearted with gentle advice, practical and relevant to each one's particular situation. Theirs was a warm, devotional faith: in one letter the Other Old Man encourages his correspondent to "Awaken the Jesus that lies asleep within" (Letter 182).[1] To another he says: "If I could fill these letters with tears and send them to you, since you have afflicted yourself, it would have been of greater benefit to you" (Letter 229).[2]

They themselves testified to their unity in Christ:

> If all of us are one (John 17.21)—the Old Man in God and I in the Old Man—then I dare to say that, if he gave you his word, I too give you mine through him. I know that I am weak and the least; yet, I cannot separate myself from the Old Man. For he is compassionate on me so that the two of us are one.[3]

Ever one in life as in death, the two Old Men of Gaza died within a year of each other around the year 543. John was the first to go to his heavenly reward, at a time he even foretold, but then postponed in response to a plea by the new abbot, Aelianos, that John first answer some questions about the administration of the monastery.

After John's death Barsanuphius went into complete seclusion in a sealed cell. Fifty years later Barsanuphius was said by some to be still alive, even though no one had seen him or brought him food in all that time, as if he had become like a Taoist immortal living for ever in the mountains gathering herbs. To allay any doubts the Patriarch of Jerusalem ordered the door of the cell of Barsanuphius to be opened by force, whereupon a fire burst out to terrify the credulous search party, driving them back to the monastery below the hill. The two Old Men, Barsanuphius and John, are commemorated together by the church on 6 February in the Eastern calendar.

Teaching silence

Although the two Old Men were recognized as gifted teachers and spiritual guides, the advice in their letters needs to be taken as responses to particular questions raised by individuals at varying stages of the spiritual path. Sometimes they would counsel different courses of action in different circumstances. They inculcated in their teaching the importance of constant vigilance over one's thoughts, commending even the kind of struggle suggested by the saying of Jesus that "the kingdom of heaven is taken by force" (see Matt 11:12). This was an emphasis not unknown in the sayings of earlier desert fathers and mothers; and yet the Old Men of Gaza qualified the need for such exertions by commending discernment in ascetic behavior. They always advocated to their correspondents the adaption of personal rules of life to their own situation, especially their state of health, exercising moderation and clarifying their motivation for action. Humility and obedience are constant monastic virtues given their place here, and they are lightened by an emphasis on gratitude and joy arising out of every situation. The labor of love, and the effort to "Bear one another's burdens, and . . . fulfil the law of Christ" (Gal 6:2), is expressed by not insisting on one's own way and by not apportioning blame. Finally, in all things, they counsel incessant tears, continuous prayer, and the delight in silence that opens the soul to God.

One typical question and response serves as a gentle introduction, and is a link to the later hesychastic teaching of John Climacus on Mount Sinai, and further back to the practice of Evagrius:

> Question: [from Andrew, an elderly and ill brother] How should one examine the thoughts? And how does one avoid the stage of captivity?
>
> *Response by Barsanuphius:*
>
> The examination of one's thoughts follows this pattern: when a thought comes, you should pay attention to what it produces. Let me give you an example. Suppose someone has insulted you, and your thought troubles you in the matter of responding. Say to your thought: 'If I respond, I disturb him and he is grieved against me. Therefore, be a little patient, and it will pass.' However, if our thought is not against some person, but thinks about evil by itself, then you must examine the thought and say: 'Where

> is this thought of evil leading?' and your thoughts will cease. Do the same in regard to all your thoughts.
>
> When the thought enters, examine it immediately and cut it short. As far as the stage of captivity is concerned, great vigilance is required. So, then, as the fathers have said, if this leads your intellect to fornication, you should lead it to sanctification. If it leads your intellect to gluttony, you should bring it to asceticism. If it leads your intellect to hatred, you should bring it to love; and so on, and so forth. Do not grieve, for you will find mercy, according to the promises that you have received. 'For if we live, we live unto the Lord; and if we die, we die unto the Lord' (Rom. 14.8).[4]

Here we have a summary of the primary method to overcome distracting thoughts in the time of prayer, or indeed at any time during the day and night. The first counsel is patience—just wait a little and the thought will dissipate of its own accord. There is no need to escalate the situation to full scale war at this stage. The obtrusive thought is cross-examined like a carefully probing investigating detective. In this way the one seeking to clear their mind quietly disidentifies with the thought. The distraction is seen as a visitor to the one at prayer, an unwanted guest to be ushered out without further ado. Particularly if the provocation comes from another person, the less said in response the better: as the saying goes, "least said soonest mended."

If the thought repeatedly comes from within then it may benefit from more examination. Where is all this leading? Is it going to be helpful to give it further energy, or is it likely to be a hindrance to your prayer? The thing to avoid if at all possible is the state of captivity, the end stage of the process of temptation outlined in the previous chapter, as taught by Mark the Ascetic and John Climacus among others. In such a case great vigilance, or watchfulness, is required to see that things do not get out of hand.

If the thought is examined with sufficient acuteness then it can be given a suitable label, such as one of the Eight Thoughts described by Evagrius, and then an appropriate remedy can be applied. Lists of vices and counteracting virtues are commonplace in this type of ascetic literature. The aspiring person of prayer is given a whole toolbox of means by which to cut off evil thoughts, complete with the sandpaper of community life to smooth off the rough edges of the psyche that remain. "Do not grieve, for you will find mercy," says Barsanuphius. His teaching is straightforward enough: "Don't get too anxious about the results of your ascetic labor. God carves us into an object of great beauty, if only we will let him. But if we are to be transformed into a work of art then be prepared to lose a few shavings along the way."

John, the Other Old Man, when asked whether a passionate thought should be rebuked angrily, points out a simpler and more direct route of escape. He acknowledges that passions are afflictions, but counsels caution in responding to their provocation. Contradicting such thoughts is only for the strong, those able to cast out demons. For us lesser mortals, says John, it is enough to flee for refuge to the Lord. Leave the exorcisms to Michael and the other archangels. It is safer just to cast yourself on the mercy of God, and to cry out to God in the name of Jesus, by which we can all be saved (Acts 4:12).[5]

Rejoicing in the Lord

Next comes a question that goes to the root of the practice of hesychasm: how to pray at all times with a pure heart and a still mind.

> Question from the same person to the same Great Old Man: Tell me, father, about unceasing prayer, and in what measure it is to be found, and whether I am obliged to have a rule.
> *Response by Barsanuphius:*
> Rejoice in the Lord, brother; rejoice in the Lord, beloved; rejoice in the Lord, fellow heir. Unceasing prayer (cf. 1 Thess. 5.17) is in accordance with the measure of dispassion. Then, the coming of the Spirit is known, and teaches us everything. If it teaches us everything, then it also teaches us about prayer. For the Apostle says: 'We do not know how to pray as we should. But the Spirit itself intercedes for us with ineffable groanings' (Rom. 8.26).

> Therefore, what should I now say to you about the buildings of Rome, when you have not yet been there? A person living in silence, especially one that is bedridden, has no rule. Therefore, be rather like a person who eats and drinks as much as he pleases. Thus, when you happen to be reading, and you see compunction in your heart, read as much as you can. Do the same when you recite the Psalms. Hold on to thanksgiving and the prayer: 'Lord have mercy,' as much as you can. And do not be afraid. 'For the gifts of God are without repentance' (Rom. 11.29).[6]

The questing monk asks about unceasing prayer, but Barsanuphius replies with a quotation from the Letter of Paul to the Philippians (4:4), exhorting him to rejoice. In the epistle this advice is given in the context of constant prayer: "Do not worry about anything, but in everything by prayer and supplication with thanksgiving let your requests be made known to God" (Phil 4:6). The Great Old Man is advocating joy above all things: "Rejoice in the Lord, beloved." Prayer is not a chore or a duty to be performed grudgingly or with self-pity. It is a response to the love of God with joy at this calling, and a trust that things will eventually work themselves out. As with most angelic visitors depicted in the Scriptures, the message is primarily one of encouragement: "Do not be afraid."

Equally, continuous prayer is based on dispassion, the *apatheia* that we discussed in Chapter 1. Equanimity, "the peace of God, which surpasses all understanding," as St. Paul goes on to say, "will guard your hearts and your minds in Christ Jesus" (Phil 4:7). This peace is both the end result and the immediate foundation of prayer, the rock on which the house of the wise man stands secure, the peace bequeathed to his bewildered disciples by the risen Christ about to ascend to his heavenly father (John 20:26). Unceasing prayer is primarily the work of the Spirit, the breath of God breathed by Jesus into his disciples as his parting gift. We do not know how to pray without ceasing, says St. Paul, but this breath of God can be a royal chariot into the presence of the risen Lord. But Barsanuphius insists that none of these descriptions are going to make much sense until you have had a taste of the actual experience of prayer without boundaries, whether of time or of space.

Using a modern metaphor he might say, "If you haven't been to Rome, how can you know what it is really like? Until you walk the streets of New York, can you know the meaning of a skyscraper? Until you have eaten a fresh mango in Africa, or a persimmon in East Asia, can you really know what these fruits taste like?"

And yet is there no hope for lesser mortals who struggle to establish a few moments of non-distraction, catching just a whiff of dispassion in their prayers? Surely for the Old Men there was an understanding of the folly of youth, as the psalmist says: "Do not remember the sins of my youth or my transgressions; according to your steadfast love, remember me, for your goodness' sake, O Lord" (Ps 25:7). All of us are the "walking wounded," catching a glimpse of the healing mercy of God in our prayers and in each other, aspiring to great heights from the top of a swaying ladder, or stuck on a stretcher in a corridor of an overwhelmed A&E. Barsanuphius acknowledges as much in his response to the question of a rule for those who are sick, asking what rule can there be. "Just make the most of your situation and do the best you can," he says. "Pray when you are able, recite the psalms when you can, give thanks and endlessly repeat, 'Lord, have mercy,' 'Kyrie eleison!' Above all, rejoice and do not be afraid. God regrets nothing of all the good things he has given us; let us not regret anything in the offering of our lives to God in return." Such is the encouragement and discernment for this suffering brother, beloved of his elders and cherished by his Lord.

Still serving

Then comes a question about silence (*hesychia*), and its relation to acts of service of others in their need.

> Question from the same brother [Dorotheus] to the same Old Man. Master, make it clear to me how I can avoid the two extremes in order to journey in the middle way. Should not certain days be explicitly set aside for silence and other days for service?
> *Response by John:*

> Neither bold in one's silence nor despising one's silence in times of distraction: such is the middle way, where one is prevented from falling by having humility in silence and vigilance in distraction, as well as by restraining one's thought. There is no limit to the hours of silence; how much more so is this the case with the days of silence. Rather, one should bear everything that comes one's way with thanksgiving. Moreover, one should suffer with all those in the monastic community, thereby fulfilling the commandment of the Apostle, namely that if one is afflicted, one should share in the affliction (1 Cor. 12.26) in order to comfort and console that person. That is what compassion is.[7]

In modern terms, this is the question of how to find a balance of action and contemplation in one's daily life. Should I ring-fence the practice of prayer, strictly keeping the hours and days I have committed myself to observe, limiting my availability for active ministry where such is required? Or should I be more flexible, and look to the needs of my neighbor rather than my own?

To this very contemporary dilemma John counsels above all humility, and flexibility in one's practice according to the principle of compassion in all things. Do not keep rigidly to your rule of life, he says, no matter how helpful you may find it to be. Outward rules are guidelines to be followed with discretion, that great virtue of the earliest desert ascetics. Be humble when distracted, not proud of your self-discipline; but equally, be vigilant, so that the fruits of your prayer are not lost when responding to a fellow human being in immediate need. Share one another's afflictions and bear everything with patience—this is the chief lesson to be learned from a lifetime's labor in the religious life. Above all be compassionate, as your father in heaven is compassionate, just as Jesus says in the Gospel (Luke 6:36-37).

Finally, there remains the question at the heart of the hesychastic tradition:

> Question. What does the sentence mean: 'Rejoice always; pray without ceasing; give thanks in all circumstances' (1 Thess. 5.16–18)?

> *Response by Barsanuphius:*
> These three things contain our entire salvation. Always rejoicing prepares the way of righteousness; for no one can truly rejoice unless one's life always appears righteous. Praying without ceasing is the aversion of every evil; for this allows no room for the devil to act against us. Finally, giving thanks in all circumstances is clear proof of our love for Christ. If the first two properly regulate our life, then we shall give thanks to the Lord.[8]

Here is the entire religious path: rejoice, pray, give thanks. Joy comes only on the basis of a clear conscience, hence the need for repentance and the value of the gift of tears, such that one knows without a shadow of doubt that one is forgiven and loved by God without measure. Unceasing prayer keeps us in this faith, trusting in God's defense and leaving no room for the accuser to act. Finally, giving thanks is not so much a command, for it cannot be manufactured or learned, only received gratefully as the blessing it truly is, leading us back into joy, and the prayer of the heart.

Watchfulness and attentiveness

Not far from Gaza, in the desert of Sinai, a monk named Hesychius became abbot of the monastery of St. Catherine. He most likely lived in the seventh century, perhaps a few decades after John Climacus, though his exact identity, and whether or not he was a priest following the Rule of St. Basil, remains unclear. Nonetheless, the teachings recorded under his name (literally "the Reverend Silence") are among the most succinct passages to be found in the whole collection of writings on hesychasm known as *The Philokalia*.

Hesychius uses the terms "watchfulness" and "attentiveness" as keystones in the architecture of his teaching. Silence is the foundation of this practice of prayerful watchfulness, the more general term that he uses in many different contexts. Watchfulness is described by Hesychius as the path to freedom, the secret passageway that leads to the mysteries of God:

> Watchfulness (*νῆψις/nepsis*) is a spiritual method which, if sedulously practised over a long period, completely frees us with God's help from impassioned thoughts, impassioned words and evil actions. It leads, in so far as this is possible, to a sure knowledge of the inapprehensible God, and helps us to penetrate the divine and hidden mysteries.[9]

Watchfulness is the virtue of self-knowledge, seeing in one's own irrefutable experience the nature of impassioned thoughts, and the words and actions that follow in their wake. It is the knowledge of causation in the spiritual and psychological realm, the patterns of which gradually become clear, as we saw in the teaching of Mark the Ascetic and John Climacus in the previous chapter. Watchfulness penetrates the mysteries of human and divine nature, seeing how these two realms of reality divide, intertwine and reunite in one life-giving whole. It is also intensely practical, embracing every virtue as people attempt to live together in harmony, in mutual love and support. It lays bare the needs of others with whom one lives, who have become partners, fellow soldiers in the struggle to be pure of heart and so to see God.

Watchfulness is complemented by the practice of attentiveness, the natural result of the practice of awareness, the fruit of a tree that has been carefully and purposefully pruned:

> Attentiveness (*προσοχή/prosochē*) is the heart's stillness, unbroken by any thought. In this stillness the heart breathes and invokes, endlessly and without ceasing, only Jesus Christ who is the Son of God and himself God.[10]

Watchfulness naturally leads to the virtue of attentiveness. The two are not easy to differentiate, but the basic sense of attentiveness here is that it is more about stillness itself, the calm after the storm of the passions has begun to subside. Attentiveness benefits greatly from the discipline of a particular focus in the practice of meditation, especially the invocation of the divine Name, which can be carried on the breath as a constant support. It can lead to a profound sense of ease and well-being, a letting go of all conflict, putting to one side for the time being the life and death struggle with afflictive impassioned thoughts.

Breathing the Lord Jesus

Some Orthodox writers express strong cautions about linking the Jesus Prayer to the rhythm of breathing where the breath is restricted following the Athonite psychosomatic technique outlined below, especially without the close supervision of a spiritual elder or guide. This way of praying the Jesus Prayer is classically described in a text attributed to Symeon the New Theologian (949–1022). There we find the following advice under the heading of *The Three Methods of Prayer*, which Symeon suggests for those who have first freed themselves from any anxiety concerning the things of this world, and who have a pure conscience by the confession of sins.

> Then sit down in a quiet cell, in a corner by yourself, and do what I tell you. Close the door, and withdraw your intellect from everything worthless and transient. Rest your beard on your chest, and focus your physical gaze, together with the whole of your intellect, upon the centre of your belly or your navel. Restrain the drawing-in of breath through your nostrils, so as not to breathe easily, and search inside yourself with your intellect so as to find the place of the heart, where all the powers of the soul reside. To start with you will find there darkness and an impenetrable density. Later, when you persist and practise this task day and night, you will find, as though miraculously, an unceasing joy. For as soon as the intellect attains the place of the heart, at once it sees things of which it previously knew nothing. It sees the open space within the heart and it beholds itself entirely luminous and full of discrimination. From then on, from whatever side a distractive thought may appear, before it has come to completion and assumed a form, the intellect immediately drives it away and destroys it with the invocation of Jesus Christ . . . The rest you will learn for yourself, with God's help, by keeping guard over your intellect and by retaining Jesus in

> your heart. As the saying goes, 'Sit in your cell and it will teach you everything.'[11]

Focusing on the navel in this way earned the practitioners of this kind of hesychastic prayer the pejorative name of "navel-gazers," a derogatory term still in use today, here implying an undue concern with individual progress, and the accompanying pride as people of prayer. For those who have sincerely prayed in this way such thoughts are just one more layer of delusion to be overcome. In any case, the idea is not to physically watch the abdomen but "to find the place of the heart, where all the powers of the soul reside." This is an exercise in what has become known as "taking the mind into the heart"—not in the sense of turning thoughts into feelings, but as a way to become familiar with the core of our being, our center of spiritual gravity, the innermost cave of the heart. And to do that you don't need to crane your neck and get terrible headaches, or even have a beard to lay against your chest! According to this method, if practiced with care, sedulously over some period of time, any initial sense of oppression and darkness will open up into a delightful feeling of openness and joy. Now there is luminosity and clear-sighted discernment as the mind and heart are united in one peaceful attentive repose. "The rest you will learn for yourself," says this author, most likely to be writing perhaps a few centuries after Symeon the New Theologian himself, even if writing in Symeon's name and "borrowing" his spiritual kudos. All hesychast teachers point out that this is not a technique but a relationship. Hesychasm is not just about the cultivation of awareness, a mindfulness of consciousness; it is also the endless invocation of the person of Jesus Christ. It is a devotional as well as an analytical practice. The analysis is needed to first clear out the clutter from the mind, in order to prepare a home for the Wisdom of God. *Hesychia*, stillness, is the preparation for a passionate invocation of the Lord, cleansing the mind, and letting the inborn radiance of the heart shine clear. This invocation can be a simple rhythmic pulse, uniting the attention with a short phrase or even a single word, finding its own rhythm as the body and mind become one. Or it can be a breathing of the holy Name, as one recent anonymous hermit says:

> When we say the Jesus prayer we fix our attention on the physical organ, on the heart, so that our attention is drawn away from the outside world and brought back again into ourselves, into the deep heart. In this way the *nous*—one of the powers of the soul—returns to its home and is united there with the other powers . . . There are some however who, from the very beginning, seek to unite the *nous* with the heart by doing breathing exercises. They breathe in the words 'Lord Jesus Christ' and exhale the words 'have mercy on me'. They follow the air as it comes into the nose all the way to the heart, and there they rest a little. This, of course, is done to allow the *nous* to be fixed on the prayer.[12]

A certain flexibility is allowable in this practice, to pray without overtiring oneself:

> If, while warming up the heart, we used thoughts about our sinfulness, it would be good, the Fathers recommend, to add the word 'sinner': 'Lord Jesus Christ, Son of God, have mercy on me a sinner.' We should stress the word to feel it more. Yet, because the *nous* can get tired of reciting the entire Jesus Prayer, it is necessary to make it shorter: 'Lord Jesus Christ, have mercy on me.' Or 'Lord have mercy on me.' Or 'Lord Jesus.' As the Christian progresses in the work of the Jesus Prayer, he can decrease the words. He can even sometimes insist on the word 'Jesus', which he says repeatedly ('Jesus, Jesus, Jesus, my Jesus') and then a wave of calmness and joy may rise in him. He should remain in this climate of sweetness which has appeared and not stop the prayer, even if his usual rule of prayer has finished. He should seize and keep this warmth of his heart and take advantage of this gift of God! For it is a great gift which God sends from on high.[13]

If preferred, one can use the name of Jesus in its Greek form, in solidarity with Christians since the foundation of the church, calling out "*Iesou*." When pronouncing the name of Jesus in Greek the emphasis falls lightly on the second half, and can be spoken internally half on the in-breath and half on the out-breath. Alternatively, it can be like a sigh, on the out-breath alone, leaving the in-breath silent and receptive, waiting for the Word to speak silently within. All such practices are best employed with the guidance of a spiritual director or accompanier. One proviso might be that if the form of prayer used becomes oppressive, or causes a feeling of tension in the chest, then it is best to leave it to one side until the experience can be shared with someone who has a wider knowledge of such practices. "Stop, look and listen before you cross the road," goes the road safety advert; the same goes for those crossing a spiritual boundary also. Such prayer is an offering of the heart, not a technique to be perfected: rather it is an attitude of openness, and a gift of the Lord.

Diligent attentiveness

Hesychius describes how watchfulness and devotion support each other:

> Watchfulness and the Jesus Prayer, as I have said, mutually reinforce one another; for close attentiveness goes with constant prayer, while prayer goes with close watchfulness and attentiveness of intellect . . . Forgetfulness can extinguish our guard over our intellect as water extinguishes fire; but the continuous repetition of the Jesus Prayer combined with strict watchfulness uproots it from our heart. The Jesus Prayer requires watchfulness as a lantern requires a candle.[14]

It is not a question of either/or, but of both/and. The attentive watchfulness of the mind is the digging of the soil, the removal of weeds and the feeding with compost; the Jesus Prayer is the multicolored flowering of the plant, and its sweet fragrance and fruitfulness.

The results of this arboreal cultivation of the mind are most commonly spoken of with the imagery of delight:

> But we sweeten it with the sense of blessed delight when in intense desire for God we practise this attention and prayer reso-

> lutely, keenly and diligently in the mind's workshop. Then we are eager to pursue stillness of heart simply for the sweetness and delight it produces in the soul.[15]

Hesychius insists that such delight can only be known at first hand in one's own experience, and yet it is available to all to some degree. It is the fruit of resolute prayer, diligently undertaken "in the mind's workshop." Like any skill it needs to be learned, while realizing also that it is a gift, and as a gift it is to be unwrapped with eagerness and delight. An eagle needs to beat its wings to climb into the sky, but once there it can glide on the warm thermal currents of air. The struggle to get "air-borne" in our prayers is the necessary precursor to the delight of contemplation. Such delight is often spoken of in terms of the radiance of an inner light, as we shall see particularly in a later chapter with reference to Symeon the New Theologian.

Walking the walk

Hesychius continues his examination of "the guarding of the intellect":

> We write of what we know; and for those who want to understand what we say, we bear witness to all that we have seen as we journey on our path . . . Those who are seized by love for this virtue . . . are enabled to become just, responsive, pure, holy and wise through Jesus Christ. Not only this, but they are able to contemplate mystically and to theologize; and when they have become contemplatives, they bathe in a sea of pure and infinite light, touching it ineffably and living and dwelling in it.[16]

Hesychius begins with the testimony that he knows what he is talking about; his advice comes from experience not conjecture. The testimony is that he has been "seized by love"—that the virtue of watchfulness has become a kind of virtuous addiction. He can no longer bear to be separated from this practice, because it is for him the source of all holiness and wisdom. It enables him "to theologize"—not that he suddenly becomes loquacious in theological discussions, but that he is enabled to catch glimpses of the divine nature itself. The workings of God, God's energies, become clear, even if God's essence remains hidden in a sea of infinite light.

From what has been said in previous chapters about the struggle with the passions, it may have seemed at times that the teaching of monastics such as John Climacus and Hesychius is a negative theology, a denigration of the feelings and the natural impulses of the heart. But just as temptation becomes an almost irresistible process with its own momentum from a lifetime's preoccupation with the self, so the whole process can be turned around from being a vicious circle to being a virtuous spiral instead. A mind preoccupied with addictive passions can, by grace, reroute the electrical cables of the self, releasing the vivacity, the innate energy of the natural state. Then afflictive passions can become effective passions of the redeemed self, able to recharge and reanimate all that makes a person truly alive.

Four types of watchfulness

Hesychius sums up the basic discipline of "watchfulness" (*νῆψις/nepsis*) as follows:

> One type of watchfulness consists in closely scrutinizing every mental image or provocation . . .
> A second type of watchfulness consists in freeing the heart from all thought, keeping it profoundly silent and still, and in praying.
> A third type consists in continually and humbly calling upon the Lord Jesus Christ for help.
> A fourth type is always to have the thought of death in one's mind.[17]

These four types of watchfulness summarize the whole of the hesychastic tradition. The first two types of watchfulness bring out the two main aspects of this practice, the two skills to be learned by anyone following this spiritual path. First there is the active guarding of the heart, scrutinizing every thought, laboriously reading the parchment of the mind. Second, there is the maintaining of that parchment pristine and clear, waiting silent and still, like a scribe poised to write the first words of inspiration as they form in the mind, looking for the moment of distillation between silence and speech, the gasp of realization. The metaphor of a scriptorium may indeed bring out the care and attention needed to succeed in these tasks, but the actual practice is more often compared to a form of warfare, like St. Paul writing in his epistles of the armor of a soldier of Christ (e.g., Eph 6:10-17). In this sense the first type of watchfulness is a kind of expansive awareness, a peripheral vision of the spirit, like a mental radar searching for threats to the mother ship of a convoy, alert to the slightest movement on the horizon. It involves the noting of thoughts as they arise, like a look-out in the crow's nest noting in his logbook all the vessels he can see, whether close by or disappearing into the haze. When necessary, this alertness of the mind can be momentarily redirected to an intruder as soon as it has been sensed, to select what evading maneuvers may be required, what mental anti-missile missile to launch, and then to return as soon as possible to a state of still and calm anticipation. It entails keeping the senses open, not getting lost in abstract thought, memories or plans for the future. It is the attentiveness of the mind or intellect (*νοῦς/nous*) to the sensations of the body and the state of the soul, just as they are, watching the thoughts and feelings come and go, directly experiencing the impermanence of all things.

The second type of watchfulness is a focused attention, concentrating on one thing above all, such as the holy Name of God, the words of a psalm or prayer, the breath in itself or as united to a prayer-word guiding the mind into the heart. The light that seems to radiate from the heart at such times may itself be the focus of meditation, filling the consciousness with a sense of being lost in the brilliancy of the divine presence (see 2 Cor 3:18). Here the multitude of passing objects of thought are largely ignored, like clouds temporarily obscuring a mountain peak, knowing that nothing needs to be done other than to wait patiently for the beauty of the mountain to be fully restored once more.

This second kind of awareness benefits from sitting still and alert, but is also helped when there is some gentle sensory stimulation to engage with: it may be the wind rustling leaves in a tree, intermittent birdsong, or the patter of rain on a windowpane; the smell of incense or flowers; the touch of a rosary or prayer rope passing through one's fingers, or a wooden cross held in the palm of one's hand. Awareness of such things keeps the mind just active enough to stave off the threat of drowsiness, and avoids losing the concentration needed to stay alert. It can lead to a profound absorption of the mind in the chosen object of meditation, accompanied by blissful bodily sensations or the arising of a clear, radiant light, which can itself become the focus of meditation.

Again, the first type of watchfulness can be compared to a wide-angle lens, keeping as much of the view as possible sharp and in focus. It opens up the overall patterns of whatever has particularly claimed our attention, experiencing the texture of the thought or sensation, seeing what effect it has on the mind. How does it feel to entertain this thought? Is it pleasurable or painful, agitated or calm? The second type of watchfulness is like a close-up lens, able to briefly capture the image of whatever has emerged into consciousness, but speedily returning to the prime focus of attention, the breath or the prayer-word.

To aid the learning of this art there are further aspects of watchfulness that can guide us along the way. The third type of watchfulness, "calling upon the Lord Jesus Christ for help," is primarily a form of the second type of focused, concentrated watchfulness, but it can also function as a default state of balance between radiant awareness and concentrated attention. This is both a resting in the love of God, savoring the lightness of the heart, the dispassion or equanimity instilled by the One who loves us beyond measure, and also an active attentiveness to the needs of others, sensing the compassion and lovingkindness, the mercy that is at work in us and all people, flowing from the love of God.

At first such prayers of devotion may seem a dualistic practice—me here in my distress and Jesus there looking down in pity—but the deeper you go the more you realize that there is no separation between the Jesus who is invoked, and the one who prays for mercy.

This realization of unity is revealed in the experience of the harmony between the two aspects of this practice, embodied in the two halves of the Jesus Prayer. This can be seen most clearly in the simplified form of the Prayer: "Lord, have mercy!" (*Κύριε ἐλέησον/Kyrie eléison*) This is an ancient supplication, in use at least since the writing of the Old Testament psalms, and sung by the earliest Christians in the Divine Liturgy. The Greek word "mercy" (*ἔλεος/eleos*) is rooted in the word for olive (*ἔλαιον/elaion*), the oil of the olive being used to soothe and heal wounds. When used in the Prayer, the invocation of the Lord is itself the invocation of mercy; even the simple physical utterance of the holy Name is an expression and a revelation of the wholeness of being. And although in its full form the Prayer may seem to end with "me, a sinner" it is in fact a way to realize the essential unity of all in Christ, who has mercy on me, through me and in the "me" that includes all of creation.

A fourth type of mindfulness, according to Hesychius, is "always to have the thought of death in one's mind." At first this may sound a morbid practice—who wants to be always thinking of death? But while the practice here includes the recommendation of visualizing the process of death, so as to fully accept its reality, that is not the usual emphasis of this teaching. Rather it is a placing of all forms of prayer and spirituality in the wider context of the inevitability of death, and in particular of accountability for actions that span the passing away of the body. Christianity has traditionally taught the "Four Last Things," that is, death, judgement, hell and heaven, remembered and anticipated in the four weeks of the season of Advent leading up to the feast of Christmas Day. "The thought of death" is an anticipation of judgement, of what it will be like to review our life in the presence of God at our final breath—whether we see that in the traditional imagery of the angelic assize at the gates of heaven, or as the life review reported by those who have had a near-death experience. All religious traditions teach that we are responsible for our actions, and will reap the rewards of our behavior, the results of the benefits or the harm we have caused others, either in this life or the next. There is no escape in death, and there will be a judgement for all to face at some time sooner or later. All actions have consequences, and it is the intention behind the actions that will be reckoned as good or evil. Life is short and death is the only inescapable certainty in life. And so, life is precious, a gift to be honored, an opportunity for "diligent stillness" at one with the Lord.

Thus, life goes on, year by year, day by day, breath by breath. It may seem that we are getting nowhere, that there is little progress to show for all our work, study and prayer. But that is our life and our salvation—just patiently dealing with the crises, small and great, that mark each and every day. To stay in the race is the mark of success, to keep watch is to be welcomed by the bridegroom when he comes.

> Human life extends cyclically through years, months, weeks, days and nights, hours and minutes. Through these periods we should extend our ascetic labours—our watchfulness, our prayer, our sweetness of heart, our diligent stillness—until our departure from this life.[18]

Questions for reflection and discussion

- Do you have a prayer-partner or spiritual director/accompanier?
- Is the practice of watchfulness or mindfulness new to you? Are they the same?
- Is the "Jesus Prayer" a practice you have found helpful?

Further reading

John Chryssavgis, 2022, *The Letters of Barsanuphius and John: Desert Wisdom for Everyday Life*, London: T&T Clark.

Lev Gillett (A monk of the Orthodox Church), 1987, 2nd edn, *The Jesus Prayer*, New York: St Vladimir's Seminary Press.

E. Kadloubovsky and G. E. H. Palmer, 1951, *Writings from the Philokalia on Prayer of the Heart*, London: Faber and Faber.

Notes

1 John Chryssavgis, 2003, *Letters from the Desert—Barsanuphius and John: A Selection of Questions and Responses*, New York: St Vladimir's Seminary Press, p. 26.

2 Chryssavgis, *Letters from the Desert*, p. 26.

3 Chryssavgis, *Letters from the Desert*, p. 13.

4 Chryssavgis, *Letters from the Desert*, p. 83.

5 Chryssavgis, *Letters from the Desert*, pp. 117–18.

6 Chryssavgis, *Letters from the Desert*, pp. 83–4.

7 Chryssavgis, *Letters from the Desert*, p. 119.

8 Chryssavgis, *Letters from the Desert*, p. 199.

9 G. E. H. Palmer, Philip Sherrard and Kallistos Ware, 1979, 1981, 1984, 1995, 2023, *The Philokalia: The Complete Text, compiled by Nikodimos of the Holy Mountain and St Makarios of Corinth*, Five Volumes, Londer: Faber, vol. 1, p. 162.

10 Palmer et al, *The Philokalia*, vol. 1, p. 163.

11 Palmer et al, *The Philokalia*, vol. 4, pp. 72–3.

12 Hierotheos, Metropolian of Nafpaktos, 1991, 3rd edn, *A Night in the Desert of the Holy Mountain: Discussion with a Hermit on the Jesus Prayer*, trans. Effie Mavromichali, Levadia: Birth of the Theotokos Monastery, p. 61.

13 Hierotheos, *A Night in the Desert*, pp. 82–3.

14 Palmer et al, *The Philokalia*, vol. 1., pp. 178–80.

15 Palmer et al, *The Philokalia*, vol. 1, p. 183.

16 Palmer et al, *The Philokalia*, vol. 1, p. 192.

17 Palmer et al, *The Philokalia*, vol. 1, pp. 164–5.

18 Palmer et al, *The Philokalia*, vol 1, p. 190.

6

Maximus the Confessor and the Centuries on Love

So far, we have outlined the beginnings of the hesychastic movement in the practice of silence and solitude. In the previous chapter we explored some of the writings of Hesychius and the two Old Men of Gaza finding them full of practical insight concerning how to pray without distraction and with an open heart. Now it is time to draw some of the threads together to reveal the consecutive steps along the path that leads to freedom and union with God. Maximus offers us the guidance of a systematic theologian, and it is to his wisdom that we now turn for further enlightenment.

Maximus the Confessor (580–662) was born into a well-off and influential family in Constantinople, the city also called Byzantium, and known now as Istanbul. Maximus is called "the Confessor" because he faithfully bore witness to his Christian faith under persecution, though without suffering direct martyrdom. From the breadth of his knowledge it is clear that Maximus received the most thorough theological education available in his day. He shows familiarity with the works of Aristotle and the neo-Platonists, as well as early church theologians such as Origen and the Cappadocian fathers: Gregory of Nazianzus, Basil of Caesarea and Gregory of Nyssa. His family gave him the contacts to enable him to move freely among the members of the intellectual and bureaucratic elite of Constantinople, and as a young man he was appointed as a secretary in the court of the emperor.

After only three years, however, Maximus left the court and moved to the monastery at Chrysopolis, where he later became abbot. The principal reason for this change of location, he said, was his desire to live an ascetic life, to engage in the true 'philosophy' of monastic discourse and endeavor. In the year 626 he left Constantinople, then in the midst of political turmoil, and went into exile in northern Africa, having stopped over at Crete on the way. Once in Africa he was drawn into theological disputes, including on the issue of whether Christ had one "will" and "activity" or two, having both a divine and a human nature. Whatever the theological merits of his case, Maximus fell foul of the political rulers of his day, being arrested by the emperor Constans II in 653. From Africa he was brought back to Constantinople, tried for heresy, condemned to have his tongue and right hand cut off (the instruments of his supposed heresy) and exiled to the south-eastern shores of the Black Sea, where he later died of his injuries.

The three powers of the soul

In his writings, Maximus draws heavily from the perspicacious teaching of Evagrius, which he combines with the warm devotion of the Macarian Homilies. Maximus highlights the two main psychological energies or sources of power, that is, desire and anger, that are felt most strongly at the early stages of the journey of faith. To these he adds the description of a third power, known as the intellect or intuition, which seeks to harness the energy of the first two more unruly energies pulling the soul in often conflicting directions. To this end he outlines some of the antidotes that can be applied to remedy each spiritual imbalance or disease. In this way Maximus uses as his framework the Platonic subdivisions of the three powers of the soul: desire (*ἐπιθυμία/epithymia*), anger (*θυμός/thumos*), and intellect (*νοῦς/nous*); or attraction, repulsion and comprehension. The terms for each of these three powers are very difficult to translate, particularly the last. Kallistos Ware gives a helpful summary:

> By 'mind' or 'intellect' (in Greek, *nous*) is meant not only or primarily the reasoning brain, with its power of discursive argumentation, but also and much more fundamentally the power of apprehending religious truth through direct insight and contemplative vision. The reason is not to be repudiated or repressed,

> for it is a faculty conferred upon us by God; but it is not the chief or the highest faculty we possess, and there are many occasions in our worship when it is transcended.[1]

The *nous*, sometimes translated as "knowledge" or "wisdom," is the governing mind that, like a charioteer, tries to keep the raging energy of the two horses of desire and aversion in check. In this analogy, which goes back to Plato in the *Phaedrus*, the chariot of the soul can keep moving speedily forward towards the goal:

> Some passions pertain to the soul's incensive power (*τὸ θυμικόν/to thymikon*) [that is, anger], and others to its desiring aspect (*τὸ ἐπιθυμιτικόν/to epithymitikon*). Both kinds are aroused through the senses. They are aroused when the soul lacks love and self-control.
>
> The passions of the soul's incensive power are more difficult to combat than those of its desiring aspect. Consequently our Lord has given a stronger remedy against them: the commandment of love.[2]

The soul is alternately pushed and pulled off course by the seemingly untrainable thoughts that plague the mind. Either we dislike something and want to be separated from it, or we desire something and cannot rest until we have made it our own. We forget the saying that there is only one thing worse than not getting what you want, and that is actually getting what you thought you wanted, only to realize, when it is finally yours, that it is not what you wanted after all!

Of the two lower powers, hatred and desire, the former is more difficult to tame, the latter being closer to the nature of the God who is himself love. According to Maximus, hatred is stirred up by the lack of love; greed is fed by the lack of self-control.

Vices and virtues

In general terms, this teaching concerning the healing of these three aspects of the self mirrors the three disciplines of fasting, almsgiving and prayer outlined by Jesus in the Sermon on the Mount (cf. Matt 6). Read in Catholic and Anglican churches each Ash Wednesday to mark the beginning of Lent, this gospel teaching of Jesus offers a practical curriculum for learning the saving grace of the commandments:

> Almsgiving heals the soul's incensive power; fasting withers the sensual desire; prayer purifies the intellect (*τὸ λογιστικόν/to logistikon*) and prepares it for the contemplation of created beings. For the Lord has given us commandments which correspond to the powers of the soul.[3]

The remedy for anger or hate is simply love, for example, in charitable almsgiving; the remedy for overpowering sensual desire is self-control, practiced, for example, in fasting. The practical wisdom of prudence balances the two, in the use of the 'intellect'—interpreted not as intelligence or deductive reasoning, but as the realization that is the fruit of immediate experience, perceived by the mind (*νοῦς/nous*) which is the eye of the heart. (In this passage, "the contemplation of created beings" is a reference to a further stage of the spiritual ascent, which we will explore later in this chapter.)

The virtue of generosity, as an antidote to anger and practiced in unobtrusive almsgiving, would seem unobjectionable, though care needs to be taken that the giver does not become proud of their generosity. "God loves a cheerful giver" (2 Cor 9:7), and cheerfulness is itself an antidote to anger. And yet, for some, anger is itself a necessary element in the battle against sin and injustice. Perhaps you don't want to be cured of this condition, even if the remedy is good enough in and of itself. Probably Maximus would respond something along the lines of: "That is all very well, but raw anger is a blunt instrument when it comes to righting wrongs." What the hesychasts like Maximus are suggesting is that the wild horses of anger and desire need to be tamed if you want to stay in the chariot to the end of the race. Halfway round a circuit of a Roman hippodrome is a very tight bend requiring great skill in order to stay upright. So it is with anger—it needs to be held tightly by the practical wisdom of prudence if it is to enable us to win the race for which the prize is eternal life.

Likewise with desire. Not everyone wants to sign up for the course of fasting if it "withers the sensual desire"! What, after all, is wrong with sensual desire? Again, the answer would be to point out the destructive side of desire, and to speak of the necessity of harnessing this immensely powerful energy securely if it is to achieve the goals it is designed to achieve. Fasting is necessary not because it will improve our figure or attractiveness (including our desire), but because over-consumption, desire gone haywire, is a scourge of every affluent society. Now more than ever the inequality induced by excessive desire needs to be remedied for the sake of the well-being of all. Fasting is not necessarily a penance: it can be a joy if it enables us to give gladly to others, to forgo an unnecessary pleasure so that someone else can be given the necessities of life. And fasting can take many forms, such as abstaining from speech, or from sources of entertainment like television or the internet.

In the end, everything is made whole by the workings of love:

> For the mind of the one who is continually with God even his concupiscence [that is, worldly desire] abounds beyond measure into a divine desire and whose entire irascible element [that is, the energy of anger] is transformed into divine love. For by an enduring participation in the divine illumination it has become altogether shining bright, and having bound its passible element [its passionate nature] to itself, as I said, turned it around to a never-ending divine desire and an unceasing love completely changing over from earthly things to divine.[4]

As we saw earlier in the teaching of Isaiah of Scetis, nothing is lost in this process. The energy native to the soul is not suppressed, simply redirected. Everything is recycled for good, reused and reapplied in a more life-giving way. The cure for "irrational desire," as Maximus calls it, is not less desire but more: rechanneling excessive love for temporal things into the irresistible desire for God. Likewise, the cure for anger and hatred of others is hatred of sin, that expresses itself as compassionate love. Thus, the twofold raging horses of attraction and repulsion, desire and disgust, while threatening to pull the chariot of the self into an avoidable heap of broken hearts and bones, are in fact able to be held in check, and the vivacity of their energy harnessed to a greater good.

This may all sound very Platonic, very Evagrian, and it is true that Maximus draws deeply from the wisdom of Evagrius, while avoiding the more speculative aspects of Origenist theology. Nonetheless, the passages where Maximus most gets into his stride are when he is talking about love (*ἀγάπη/agāpe*) rather than about knowledge (*γνῶσις/gnōsis*), even though he continues to acknowledge both as essential foundations of a spiritual life.

Four Centuries on Love

The most well-known and most accessible of the works of Maximus are the *Four Centuries on Love*. These four collections of pithy sayings comprise a hundred sentences or paragraphs, following a meandering path that, read slowly and with patient attention, reveal a clear way forward in a confusing world. Reading them is like following a stream through a wood, occasionally tripping over a protruding tree root, but finally reaching a still pond that opens out to the sky. The *First Century* of Maximus begins with a definition of love:

> Love is a holy disposition of the soul, in accordance with which it values knowledge of God above all created things. We cannot attain lasting possession of such love while we are still attached to anything worldly.
>
> Dispassion engenders love, hope in God engenders dispassion, and patience and forbearance engender hope in God; these in turn are the product of complete self-control, which itself springs from fear of God. Fear of God is the result of faith in God.[5]

Maximus traces the virtues back to their ultimate origin in a kind of backstitch pattern, but perhaps it is easier to see the sequence from beginning to end. So here we have faith in God → fear of God

→ self-control → patience and forbearance → hope in God → dispassion → love. Faith in God is one of the "three theological virtues" spoken of by St. Paul (1 Cor 13:13), together with hope and love (and "love never ends," v. 8). Fear of God is "the beginning of wisdom" (Prov 9:10), referring not to a debilitating anxiety, but to a sense of reverence at the awe-inspiring mystery of God. Self-control is the ability to regulate destructive impulses, to pause before responding, to act rather than just react. It is itself a kind of patience and forbearance, directed towards oneself as much as others. All of this leads to dispassion, the "*apatheia*" we have come across so often in these pages. Maximus himself marks this out with special attention in his preliminary remarks. Downplaying "attachment to anything worldly" is likely to be a stumbling block for many modern readers, but it is important to point out once more that this virtue of dispassion carries the meaning of equanimity, reintegration and spiritual freedom. It was translated into Latin by John Cassian in the fourth century as *puritas cordis*, purity of heart. As such it is that by which God is seen and known (Matt 5:8) and is described here by Maximus as the immediate precursor to love.

The love spoken of here is that denoted by the Greek word *ἀγάπη* (*agāpe*), the love or affection described by St. Paul in 1 Corinthians 13 as patient and kind, generous and forgiving. It used to be translated as "charity" before that term became more narrowly defined as a gift to a particular good cause. This love spoken of by Maximus is praised above all as a "disposition of the soul," a readiness to act rather than just a static sense of being. It "values knowledge of God," that is, the direct experience of the presence of God. This experience of divinity is not in contradistinction to created things, but is found in and through and above all things. Dispassion, a very Evagrian term, is about catching a glimpse of the wordless wonder of the soul's ultimate ascent/descent into God. But Maximus goes further than Evagrius in his encomium of love. This kind of love is the natural radiance of the mind:

> As the light of the sun attracts the healthy eye, so does the knowledge of God draw the pure mind to itself naturally through love.

> The mind is pure when it is removed from ignorance and illuminated by divine light.
>
> The soul is pure when it has been freed from the passions and rejoices unceasingly in divine love.
>
> A blameworthy passion is a movement of the soul contrary to nature.
>
> Detachment is a peaceful state of the soul in which it becomes resistant to vice.[6]

This detachment is a joyful, expansive state of equanimity, which can be described as a resting in the compassion of God. It is the most natural thing in the world—not a construct of the mind, but a deconstruction of the selfish self. It is a reflection of the self-emptying love of the Son of God, "who, though he was in the form of God, did not regard equality with God as something to be exploited, but emptied himself, taking the form of a slave, being born in human likeness" (Phil 2:6-7). This is described by Maximus in his commentary *On the Lord's Prayer* as *kenosis* (*κένωσις*), the self-emptying of the incarnation:

> The Logos [the Word of God] bestows adoption on us when he grants us that birth and deification which, transcending nature, comes by grace from above through the Spirit. The guarding and preservation of this in God depends on the resolve of those thus born; on their sincere acceptance of the grace bestowed on them and, through the practice of the commandments, on the cultivation of the beauty given to them by grace. Moreover, by emptying themselves of the passions they lay hold of the divine to the same degree as that to which, deliberately emptying himself of his own sublime glory, the Logos of God truly became man.[7]

Although Maximus insists that the Christian life, in particular the practice of stillness and silence, is cultivated by the hard work of ascetic discipline, still he acknowledges that whatever gains may be made, whatever insights achieved, whatever transformation of consciousness may be attained, still it is all grace, all is a gift of God. Furthermore, the self-emptying detachment of Christians is analogous to the self-emptying of Jesus: as the Word of God descends from heaven and becomes human, so humanity is born again and is "divinized" by love, that they "may become participants in the divine nature" (2 Pet 1:4). Or as St Athanasius (c. 296–373) put it most succinctly several centuries before: "God became human that humanity might become God."[8]

Christ is everything and is in everything

Maximus is convinced that the self-emptying love of Christ, seen in the letting go of all grasping, is the path of salvation. It constitutes the remodeling of the fall of humanity into a self-emptying obedience to God, and is naturally exhibited by unity between all the members of humanity:

> The one who is perfect in love and has reached the summit of detachment knows no distinction between one's own and another's, between faithful and unfaithful, between slave and freeman, or indeed between male and female. But having risen above the tyranny of the passions and looking to the nature of [humanity] he regards all equally and is equally disposed toward all. For in him there is neither Greek nor Jew, neither male nor female, neither slave nor freemen, but Christ is everything and in everything.[9]

This unitive vision echoes that of St. Paul writing to the Galatians (Gal 3:28). It is one of the central pillars of Paul's teaching, and one that most often got him into trouble. It is based on his insight into the Body of Christ (see 1 Cor 12), in which all members of the body are of equal merit and deserve equal honor. Indeed, the less honorable parts deserve the greatest respect. But following on from these insights is the great passage on love in 1 Corinthians 13 already alluded to, and Maximus is keen to make this his own manifesto, while gently acknowledging the frailty of human relationships and the need to adapt one's behavior to one's ability at the time of trial:

> Be as eager as you can to love [everyone], but if you cannot do this yet, at least do not hate anyone . . . Such a one has offended

> you; do not hate him but rather the offense and the demon who contrived the offense. If you hate the offender, you hate a person and transgress the commandment, and what he did in word you do in deed. But if you keep the commandment, give proof of your love, and if you in any way can, help him so that he can be delivered from wickedness.
>
> Christ does not want you to have hate for anyone, or grief, or anger, or resentment in any way at all or for any temporal reason whatsoever. And this is thoroughly proclaimed in the four Gospels.[10]

But it is not just about the relationships between people and accepting all as brothers and sisters in God's family—it is also about being able to cultivate a sense of equanimity whatever life throws at you, not as a passive resignation but as an active expression of love:

> If you are not indifferent to both fame and dishonour, riches and poverty, pleasure and distress, you have not yet acquired perfect love. For perfect love is indifferent not only to these but even to this fleeting life and to death.[11]

Whenever you are praised, says Maximus, watch out! It won't be long before the natural balance of nature re-rights itself and a corresponding blame echoes in your ears. Don't put your trust in money, tomorrow the stock market could collapse. Whatever you like will become otherwise; whatever you run from will catch you up in the end.

Contemplating nature

For the hesychasts, love and knowledge are intimately inter-related. To put it more forthrightly, true knowledge of God and your neighbor is impossible without love. The ever-widening path of knowledge is mapped out by a classification held in common by both Evagrius and Maximus. Back in the fourth century, Evagrius of Pontus, in his *Kephalaia Gnostika (Gnostic Chapters)*, defined the spiritual path in the following enigmatic words:

> While transformations are many, we have received the knowledge of only four (of them): of the first, of the second, of the last, and of the penultimate. And the first is, as has been said, the passage from evil to virtue, whereas the second is that from impassivity to the secondary natural contemplation (*θεωρία φυσικὴ/theoria phusike*), and the third is that from the latter to the knowledge concerning rational creatures, and the fourth is the passage of all to the knowledge of the Holy Trinity.[12]

The first stage is that of the practical purification of the mind from every evil thought and tendency in the mind. We have seen this in the teaching of many of the hesychasts. It is the recognition and elimination of the afflictive passions, and their substitution with the corresponding virtues using the innate powers of the soul, as described by Maximus in the earlier part of this chapter.

This leads to impassivity or dispassion as the basis for understanding the true nature of all things and their purpose in the divine dispensation, the reasons (*λόγοι/logoi*) for their existence. This is explained by Evagrius in an earlier paragraph:

> In the secondary natural contemplation (*θεωρία φυσικὴ/theoria phusike*) we see Christ's Wisdom, full of varieties, that which he used and in which he created the worlds/aeons, whereas in the knowledge that is about rational creatures we have been instructed concerning his substance.[13]

The "secondary natural contemplation" he terms "physics" (*φυσικὴ*), ironically so, as the modern definition of physics as the scientific study of matter and energy is thought by many to have disproved, or at least made unnecessary, the doctrine of the existence of God. In the teaching of Evagrius and Maximus, however, natural contemplation is the observance of the natural world from the viewpoint of faith, as if seeing the blueprints, the architect's plans, for each individual thing in creation. This includes knowledge of inanimate things by secondary natural contemplation, and also by primary natural contemplation, understanding all rational creatures, whether human or angelic. Finally, knowledge of the Holy Trinity is attained and one is caught up in union with God.

Maximus gives his summary of the practice of natural contemplation as follows:

> When the mind is completely freed from the passions, it journeys straight ahead to the contemplation of created things and makes its way to the knowledge of the Holy Trinity.[14]

And again, expanding the pattern to a fourfold analysis, he says:

> Through the working out of the commandments the mind puts off the passions. Through the spiritual contemplation of visible realities it puts off impassioned thoughts of things. Through the knowledge of invisible realities it puts off contemplation of visible things. And finally this it puts off through the knowledge of the Holy Trinity.[15]

For Maximus natural contemplation is a steady unveiling of the true nature of things, gradually moving from the visible to the invisible, the impermanent to the eternal, the human to the divine.

Theologian Adam Cooper explains the purpose of Maximus' doctrine of the *logoi* in the practice of "natural contemplation":

> The doctrine of the *logoi* articulates the double reality of the simultaneous distinction and relation between God the Logos and the manifold created beings. For every species or generic category of created being—whether visible or invisible, angelic or human—there is a corresponding *logos* or divine rationale that determines its nature and function—determines and qualifies, that is, 'what' that thing is or should be, since it is in accordance with the respective generic *logoi* that God distributes particular existence through the hierarchy of highest to lowest forms of being . . . All created beings, therefore, participate in God in so far as they have being from him corresponding to the *logoi*.[16]

The *logoi*, the ideas or plans that God has for everything in creation, pre-exist in the mind of God. The *logoi* are "a portion of God," in the daring phrase coined by Gregory Nazianzus and taken up again by Maximus. They are God's intentions regarding creation, the benign algorithms that coordinate our coming to be: not sketches on the back of a proverbial cigarette packet, but patterns akin to DNA in the "cells" of God that reproduce in the contingent being of all created things.

Because all things exist by sharing in the being of God, all things reveal something of the divine nature—they are "theophanic," they make God visible. This means that everything that exists is immensely precious. We are all part of the divine genome. If some segments of DNA become corrupted or are excised, then the whole is diminished, possibilities become impossible, and nature is irrevocably diminished. Each *logos*, each guiding principle that can be used for good is in itself a treasure to be stored and used creatively. Each thing is an individual color on the divine palette, a unique fleeting fragrance of this flower garden earth, a never to be repeated combination of spice and seasoning in the kitchen of the banquet of heaven. Everything images God, reveals God, makes God tangible and real.

This infinite variety of creation such that everything is unique and irreplaceable is something that the medieval Franciscan scholar John Duns Scotus would later call *haecceitas*, "thus-ness," and the nineteenth-century poet Gerard Manley Hopkins would call "inscape." As Hopkins wrote in his poem "As kingfishers catch fire":

> Each mortal thing does one thing and the same:
> Deals out that being indoors each one dwells;
> Selves—goes itself; *myself* it speaks and spells,
> Crying *Whát I dó is me: for that I came.*[17]

"Natural contemplation" is a discovery of the coming to be of all things in the present moment, an insight into their fragility and yet their endurance, being held in being by the Being of God. It is an awareness of the pulse of life, the wonder of existence, revealing itself most often when the senses are heightened after a lengthy time of silent meditation. It is not an achievement after the labor of prayer, but a letting go of all sense of personal achievement, being in itself a work of grace. As such, it is a revelation and a conviction of the essential goodness of all things—their being and their virtue.

Maximus illustrates this by quoting from the book of Genesis: "Then God said, 'Let us make humankind in our image, according to our likeness' " (Gen 1:26). Humanity, being made out of nothing and inherently transient, is nonetheless made by grace in the image of God. By this we share in the being of God: having nothing of our own, we are breathed-into, like the first human being raised from the dust of the earth. This image of God within us is the foundation of our being, most eloquently expressed by the gasp of surprise that we should exist at all. On this foundation we are molded into the likeness of God by the patient chipping away of the divine chisel, as the virtues are formed and ingrained in our very being.

And it is not just the soul that is the beneficiary of this process. The entire human person, body and soul, shares in this redemption, this well-being of God. Although it may sound to our modern ears that Maximus is at times denigrating the body and encouraging us to abandon the flesh and take flight to some ethereal heaven bereft of the unreasoning body, in actuality, according to Maximus, body and soul are inseparably united in the gift of salvation:

> God directs them [soul and body] towards what he thinks fit and fills them with his own glory and blessedness, graciously giving them unending and ineffable life . . . [This is] God entire being participated in by all: God entire becoming to the soul—and through the mediation of the soul, to the body—what the soul is to the body, as he himself knows how, so that the soul receives immutability and the body immortality. Thus the whole human being, as the object of divine action, is deified by the grace of the God who became a human being. He remains wholly human in both soul and body by nature, yet becomes wholly God in soul and body by grace and by the divine radiance of the blessed glory, a radiance appropriate to him, beside which nothing more radiant and exalted can be imagined.[18]

Just in case the reader missed the audacity of this teaching, let it be pointed out that the subject of the last sentence is "the whole human being." Humanity becomes human, by letting the grace of God mold both body and soul into one exalted reality, full of the radiance of

God's glory. This is the teaching of divinization (*θέωσις/theosis*), a central teaching of the Orthodox Church even today. And this is where we loop back into the undergirding theme of this book: silence and its role in prayer and contemplation.

Pure prayer and the divine and infinite light

In his *Four Centuries on Love*, Maximus hints at something that happens in pure imageless prayer beyond the revelations of natural contemplation—the summit of deification (*theosis*) in a blaze of light:

> There are two supreme states of pure prayer, one corresponding to those of the active life, the other to the contemplatives. The first arises in the soul from the fear of God and an upright hope, the second from divine desire and total purification. The marks of the first type are the drawing of one's mind away from all the world's considerations, and as God is present to one, as indeed he is, he makes his prayers without distraction or disturbance. The marks of the second type are that at every onset of prayer the mind is taken hold of by the divine and infinite light and is conscious neither of itself nor of any other being whatever except of him who through love brings about such brightness in it. Then, when it is concerned with the properties of God, it recites impressions of him which are clear and distinct.[19]

This passage reduces the higher stages of the spiritual journey to two phases, two types of "pure prayer." The first is characterized by desire for God and purification of the mind; the second is a letting go of all particular considerations and a focusing instead on the experience of light, being overwhelmed by the brightness of the infinite radiance of God. It is as if those practicing this latter form of prayer step directly into an icon of the Transfiguration of Christ on Mount Tabor and are themselves transfigured by uncreated light. The disciples then, and those who pray now, are surrounded and suffused with this light. At first a dark cloud envelops the mountain, but then the darkness is dissolved in light within which all else is swallowed up and forgotten.

Although obviously an intensely personal experience, this transfiguration also involves a dissolving of the separate self and a loss of ego-centered boundaries. This is a theme dear to the heart of the sixth-century Syrian author who writes under the name of Dionysius the Areopagite. Maximus was clearly deeply influenced by the writings of Dionysius, particularly *The Ecclesiastical Hierarchy* and *The Mystical Theology*. In the latter, Dionysius begins with a hymn of praise, which illustrates the way he likes to improvise playfully with the themes of light and darkness:

> Trinity!! Higher than any being,
> any divinity, any goodness!
> Guide of Christians
> in the wisdom of heaven!
> Lead us up beyond unknowing and light,
> up to the farthest, highest peak of mystic scripture,
> where the mysteries of God's Word
> lie simple, absolute and unchangeable
> in the brilliant darkness of a hidden silence.
> Amid the deepest shadow
> they pour overwhelming light
> on what is most manifest.
> Amid the wholly unsensed and unseen
> they completely fill our sightless minds
> with treasures beyond all beauty.[20]

All is revealed in "the brilliant darkness of a hidden silence"—the mind freed from all images in contemplative prayer—as the overwhelming divine light is poured out. Dionysius continues:

> Here, renouncing all that the mind may conceive, wrapped entirely in the intangible and the invisible, he belongs completely to him who is beyond everything. Here, being neither oneself nor someone else, one is supremely united by a completely unknowing inactivity of all knowledge, and knows beyond the mind by knowing nothing.[21]

To know by knowing nothing, or to realize that no-thingness, no objectification, is the highest knowledge, is to discover the God who is above all categories, even of being itself. And this is not a ticket to religious stardom. All pretensions of a secret knowledge that can be articulated only by the seer—a kind of possession of sacred truth—are swept away. The woman or man of prayer is neither themselves nor another, and knows by unknowing, acting in the complete stillness of a mind that knows nothing (and knows everything that can be known!) It is a discourse with hardly any positive content, but then that is the point. It is a kind of mirror-image of whatever is said or asserted otherwise, like anti-matter to the matter of theology. It is language which is designed to cancel out language, and to leave the simple realization of the experience of the presence of God (something many philosophers of religion would deny is possible).

Stewards of the sacred mysteries

This experience of the divine emptiness is portrayed by Dionysius, and by Gregory of Nyssa before him, as the experience of Moses on Mount Sinai, but it is really the summit of the experience of *hesychia*—stillness and silence—the mystery of which is the subject of this book.

This is not the silence of isolation, a silence experienced only in physical solitude. It is a silence (and a theology) that can be experienced daily in the church that is the body of Christ. Divinization is enacted each time the sacred mysteries of the Eucharistic liturgy are celebrated, and the body and blood of the Lord intimately received. In his work *The Church's Mystagogy*, Maximus describes this moment of the liturgy in the most exalted words:

> The blessed invocation of the great God and Father and the acclamation of the 'One is holy' and what follows and the partaking of the holy and life-giving mysteries signify the adoption and union, as well as the familiarity and the divine likeness and deification which will come about through the goodness of our God in every way on all the worthy, when God himself will be 'all in

all' alike to those who are saved as a pattern of beauty resplendent as a cause in those who are resplendent along with him in grace by virtue and knowledge.[22]

This somewhat breathless sentence gives a flavor of the nature of deification. In this treatise Maximus goes through the entire liturgy, explaining how each area of the church, each liturgical action and symbolic gesture, expresses some aspect of the unity of humanity, body and soul, itself being indwelt by the living God. And it is not just about humanity—the liturgy is about making tangible the divine activity uniting all heaven and earth, the whole cosmos being divinized, irradiated with divine light, being none other than the body of God, as the soul and body of each individual human being is one.

The biblical basis for this teaching of the transformation of humanity by the light of Christ is found both in the Gospels and in Paul's epistles. Maximus points to Paul's experiences of the divine light alluded to in his Second Letter to the Corinthians, in a discourse about the shining face of Moses as he descends from the mountain having seen and talked with God; so Paul says of Christians: "And all of us, with unveiled faces, seeing the glory of the Lord as though reflected in a mirror, are being transformed into the same image from one degree of glory to another; for this comes from the Lord, the Spirit" (2 Cor 3:18). Maximus is keen to point out that this all "comes from the Lord": all is grace, the gift of God. As Paul writes to the Galatians: "it is no longer I who live, but it is Christ who lives in me" (Gal 2:20). The one who acts is Christ; Paul is lost in faith and love of God. Another favorite text of Maximus is the mysterious saying of Jesus in the Gospel of John: "Is it not written in your law, 'I said, you are gods'?" (John 10:34). Here Jesus is quoting Psalm 82:6, implying that his hearers should be acting as true gods, that is, beings with the power to govern the nations of the earth with wisdom and justice. The irony in the question about being gods in John's Gospel is that Jesus is himself being criticized by the theologians of his day for making himself out to be God. In response he is saying in effect that we are all gods in God's eyes, so how can he, Jesus, be exempt from this restoration of the divine image, this superimposition of the likeness of God?

Thus, Maximus the Confessor leads us into the mysteries of the love of God. He begins with the purification of the mind—the exploration of the powers of the soul and their training by the wisdom that recognizes virtue and vice, and the skillful and unskillful hand of the charioteer in the race to ultimate victory. Then, as the mind gains greater clarity of spiritual vision, the secrets of nature are revealed, and in contemplating creation the Creator becomes visible to the eye of faith. Finally, the soul is transformed such that its innate divinity is made known, and God and humanity are revealed to be one reality, one joy, one light, one person, one love. To take us deeper into that love we now turn to the overflowing love and compassion of Isaac of Syria.

Questions for reflection and discussion

- Does the teaching of the three powers of the soul make sense of your own experience?
- Which is more important—knowledge of God or love of God? Are they different?
- Do you find God in the contemplation of nature?

Further reading

John Anthony McGuckin, 2001, *Standing in God's Holy Fire: The Byzantine Tradition*, Traditions of Christian Spirituality Series, London: Darton, Longman & Todd.

George C. Berthold, 1985, *Maximus the Confessor—Selected Writings*, Classics of Western Spirituality, London: SPCK.

John Chryssavgis, 2013, with Bruce V. Foltz (ed.), *Toward an Ecology of Transfiguration: Orthodox Christian Perspectives on Environment, Nature, and Creation*, New York: Fordham University Press.

Notes

1 Bishop Kallistos Ware, 2001, *The Inner Kingdom, Volume 1 of the Collected Works*, New York: St Vladimir's Seminary Press, p. 61.

2 G. E. H. Palmer, Philip Sherrard and Kallistos Ware, 1979, 1981, 1984, 1995, 2023, *The Philokalia: The Complete Text, compiled by St Nikodimos of the Holy Mountain and St Makarios of Corinth*, Five Volumes, London: Faber, vol. 2, pp. 59–60.

3 Palmer et al, *The Philokalia*, vol. 2, pp. 61–2.

4 *Centuries on Love (CL)* 2.48. George C. Berthold, 1985, *Maximus the Confessor—Selected Writings*, Classics of Western Spirituality, London: SPCK, pp. 53–4.

5 *Centuries on Love (CL)* 1.1–2; Andrew Louth, 1996, *Maximus the Confessor*, London: Routledge, p. 38.

6 *CL* 1.32-36; Berthold, *Maximus*, pp. 38–9.

7 Louth, *Maximus*, pp. 33–4.

8 See Jules Gross, 2002, *The Divinization of the Christian: According to the Greek Fathers*, Anaheim, CA: A&C Press, pp. 166–9.

9 *CL* 2.30; Berthold, *Maximus*, p. 51.

10 *CL* 4.82–84; Berthold, *Maximus*, pp. 84–5.

11 *CL* 1.72; Palmer et al, *The Philokalia*, vol. 2, p. 61.

12 Ilaria L. E. Ramelli, 2015, *Evagrius, Kephalaia Gnostika: A New Translation of the Unreformed Text from the Syriac*, Atlanta, GA: Society of Biblical Literature Press, p. 89.

13 Ramelli, *Kephalaia Gnostika*, p. 85.

14 *CL* 1.86; Berthold, *Maximus*, p. 45.

15 *CL* 1.94; Berthold, *Maximus*, p. 45.

16 Adam G. Cooper, 2005, *The Body in St Maximus the Confessor: Holy Flesh, Wholly Deified*, Oxford Early Christian Studies, Oxford: Oxford University Press, p. 94.

17 *The Poems of Gerard Manley Hopkins*, 1970, 4th edn, ed. W. H. Gardner and N. H. MacKenzie, Oxford: Oxford University Press, p. 90.

18 Maximus quoted in Cooper, *The Body*, p. 101.

19 *CL* 2.6; Berthold, *Maximus*, p. 47.

20 Colm Luibheid, 1987, *Pseudo-Dionysius: The Complete Works*, Classics of Western Spirituality, New York: Paulist Press, p. 135.

21 Luibheid, *Pseudo-Dionysius*, p. 137.

22 Berthold, *Maximus*, p. 210.

7

Isaac of Syria and the Ocean of God's Mercy

Born in 1853 in north-western Persia, in what is now Iran, Yaroo Neesan was on a mission to save the precious heritage of his beloved Syrian church, rescuing priceless manuscripts from ransacked churches and monasteries and bringing them to safety. One collection he deposited at the Bodleian Library of the University of Oxford in 1898 while on leave in England. There it stayed, boxed, labelled and hidden from view for a hundred years, identified as "MS.syr.e.7." In 1983, casting his eyes over the intriguing catalogue title of this unknown Syriac document, Professor Sebastian Brock of the university's Oriental Institute requested that it be brought up from storage in the library archives. He tells the story of the discovery in his own words:

> I was there collating a manuscript against a printed text for someone and had got rather bored. Seeing that I needed a break, I leafed through the card index of uncatalogued Oriental manuscripts in the Bodleian. My eye caught on one that had something like 'Isaac of Nineveh, c. 11th century'. It was probably the early date that primarily suggested to me it would be fun to order it up. I wondered: it might have a colophon [an inscription at the end of a manuscript] saying where it was written. It did! An hour or so later it appeared, a small tightly bound volume on parchment in an East Syriac hand, of the approximate date on the card. It had lost its beginning, but I saw that in the colophon it said it was 'the second half' of Isaac's writings. I could not at the time remember which half was already known, so it was not till I got home and looked the details up that I found out that it was indeed the lost part—that had sat in the Bodleian for just about

> a century undetected! . . . so as much as possible of vacations for the next ten years were spent preparing the edition and translation.[1]

Isaac, now known as St. Isaac of Syria, was in fact born in Qatar in the Persian Gulf. The exact dates of his birth and death are not known, but it is thought that he lived sometime in the seventh century. He is also known as Isaac of Nineveh (now Mosul in Iraq), where he briefly served as bishop. According to one ancient Arabic source, on the very first day after his consecration, two argumentative Christians, squabbling over the repayment of a loan, dissipated his episcopal patience by each one demanding that Isaac rule in their favor. "Just follow the gospel teaching not to take back what has been given away!" Isaac cried out. "Never mind the gospel!" was their reply, which was the cue for Isaac to believe he was definitely in the wrong place, and so he headed straight back to a hermitage in the mountainous region of Beit Huzaye.

For someone who lived much of his adult life as a hermit monk in arid areas, water and the sea are the source of many of the rich images and similes of his writings. He compares the spiritual journey to a voyage across the ocean of God's love, the staging posts being islands along the way. The discovery of the Kingdom of God is like a diver nearly bursting his lungs in search for pearls, and finding one with great joy. The freedom of the Christian life is to Isaac like the play of dolphins in tropical waters.

As well as dreaming of the sea, Isaac also loved books, and read and wrote so much that, according to one source, he ended his life blind. He even compared the spiritual life to the process of writing and editing a manuscript:

> As long as we are in the place where altering is possible, let us observe ourselves; and while we have authority over our life-book and our book is still between our hands, let us zealously add acts of beautiful behaviour, and let us scratch from it the loss of the old behaviour without freedom. We are allowed to scratch out faults, as long as we are here. And God will take into account every alteration we make in it. May we be deemed

> worthy of life everlasting before we appear before the king, and he puts his seal on the book.[2]

Before the widespread use of paper, books were usually made of dried and stretched animal hide such as calfskin. Mistakes by the scribe could be corrected by re-scraping the vellum or parchment. Only rich individuals or institutions could afford such books, the idea of a "life-book" perhaps suggesting the importance of each human life to God, who cares about every individual person.

The call to "observe ourselves" in the passage above is an initial link between the Syrian tradition and those of Egypt and Palestine which we have already been exploring. Isaac outlines some of the many forms this watchfulness can take, and how they arise out of stillness, all recorded in the previously lost Second Part of his writings.

> Just as there is nothing which resembles God, so there is no ministry or work which resembles converse with God in stillness. What is conversation with God? This meditation and converse (directed) towards God has many paths, each person (taking) the path for which his understanding is capable and on which he (can) make progress, drawing closer to God on it as a result of daily experience. A person will travel on any one of these paths in accordance with his measure, so that thereby he may find joy with God, and be filled in his intellect and in his meditation with the recollection of Him at all times.[3]

Isaac does not insist that there is only one way to God. The relationship with God is like a conversation that over time comes to a mutual understanding, rather than a monologue with no opportunity for debate. And yet such a conversation is held more in stillness than in sound. For Isaac, stillness underlies everything. It is out of silence that words emerge, if they are to be words of life. Every path is unique, and each one is adapted to the ability and daily realities of a person's life. The only thing that is recommended to all is the desire to pray without ceasing, to be filled with the recollection of God in all circumstances.

The solitary at prayer

Nonetheless, Isaac is a convinced monk and solitary, living a life of extreme simplicity alone or in the company of a few like-minded ascetics. He writes as a monk for monks, and the practical suggestions he makes assume this basic pattern of life. For those particularly set on the path of contemplative prayer in a monastic environment the recollection of the presence of God in all circumstances can happen in various time-hallowed ways. These include reading Scripture, reciting the Psalter, chanting the Daily Office, the seven daily "hours" of prayer from Lauds to Compline, dawn till dusk.

Posture is important too. Some find it helpful to stand in prayer with outstretched arms, or kneeling and prostrating oneself in the way that Muslims and Orthodox Christians continue to do to this day. Prayers can be "said" in many non-verbal ways, such as making the sign of the cross, or standing with arms outstretched. Furthermore, any kind of simple manual work can form the background to the silent recitation of verses from the Psalms or the continual recollection of God, and that is why manual work such as wood-carving or icon painting has often been the means of monastic self-support. But you don't need to be a monk to carve a crucifix out of wood, and the quiet of a workshop can be as solemn and sacred as a remote hermitage chapel.

But this labor of prayer in all occupations is not the summit of the path, merely the hard work of rowing a becalmed spiritual ship, or maneuvering it into a harbor. When the spirit blows more strongly, and the wind rises in the sails, then progress is altogether more marked:

> In the life of the spirit, on the other hand, there is no (longer any) prayer. Every kind of prayer that exists (consists of) beauteous thoughts, and these are stirrings on the level of the soul. On the level of the life of the spirit, there are no thoughts, no stirrings; no, not even any sensation or the slightest movement of the soul concerning anything, for (human) nature completely departs from these things and from all that belongs to itself. (Instead) it remains in a certain ineffable and inexplicable silence,

> for the working of the Holy Spirit stirs in it, it being raised above the realm of the soul's understanding.
>
> What then shall we say? Where thoughts do not exist, who can speak any longer of prayer—or of anything else?[4]

Prayer, for Isaac, is a mode of travel that is no longer needed once the harbor, the "ineffable and inexplicable silence" of God, has been reached. This raises an intriguing question: When I am no longer thinking, no longer explaining my actions by telling stories to myself or others, then who am I? If I do not define myself, does that mean I am lost and abandoned, or that I have finally let go of demarcations of where I begin and where I cease to be? Loving-kindness does not automatically construct the self; it is the sense of grievance, or the cherished grudge of resentment, that solidifies myself as a person wronged. When I am just the awareness of the pain and happiness of others, have I abandoned myself, or have I finally discovered who I am?

The ocean of stillness

It is in describing the sea of stillness that Isaac finds the wind in his sails first flap and then fill the canvas, such that the skiff of his contemplation noiselessly pulls at the tiller in his hands:

> As the eyes of the helmsman look to the stars, so the solitary throughout the whole course of his journey looks, with the inner eye of divine vision, to the goal which he fixed in his mind from the first day when he gave himself to voyaging over the billowy sea of stillness, until he discovers that pearl for the sake of which he set off into the unfathomable deep of the ocean of stillness. The watchful gaze of his expectation makes light for him the heavy burden of his labour and the perilous hardships which befall him on his way.[5]

Isaac is aware that the journey is dangerous to life and limb, and yet the labor yields much fruit, the spoils of trade (his life for his

Lord) demanding the initial loss of all things and yet promising the ineffable rewards of eternal life.

For Isaac, the basis of the higher reaches of prayer is nothing but stillness, and the joy that surges over him as he enters into the silence of wonder:

> I run to stillness so that the verses of my reading and prayer should be sweet to me. And when my tongue is silent because of the sweetness that comes from understanding them, then, as it were into a kind of sleep, I fall into a state where my senses and my thoughts become inactive. When from prolonged stillness waves of joy ceaselessly surge over me, waves arising from inward stirrings that beyond expectation suddenly pour abroad to delight my heart. And when these waves approach the barque of my soul, they plunge her into veritable wonders in the stillness which is in God, taking her far from the whisperings of the world and the life of the flesh.[6]

Stillness is not a restriction of movement, nor silence an enforced absence of sound—rather, both are the gifts of the invisible spirit that fills our hearts with praise and our minds with wonder. The labor of watchfulness is necessary to tow us out beyond the shallows of our prayers, but ultimately it is awe (not oars!) that propels us into the mystery of God, and that brings us safely to the harbor for which we long:

> When the power of stillness overshadows you on account of prolonged abiding in your cell, laborious works, watchfulness over hidden things, and restraint of the senses from every encounter, then at first you will find a joy which without cause overcomes your soul at times and seasons; and thereupon according to the degree of your purity your eyes will be opened to see God's creative power and the beauty of created things. And when the mind is guided by the wonder of this divine vision, then night and day will be as one to it, because of its awe at the glorious creations of God. Hereafter the awareness of the passions is stolen from the very soul herself by the sweetness of this divine vision.[7]

Here, "restraint of the senses" leads to the purity of vision that sees through materiality to "the beauty of created things." This is the natural contemplation that Evagrius and Maximus the Confessor wrote about. It is characterized by wonder and delight.

Repentance, purity and perfection

In one of his *Ascetical Homilies*, Isaac summarizes his teaching on the spiritual voyage in three words: repentance, purity and perfection. First, repentance is the avoidance of sin and the cultivation of virtue, the wrestling with the vagaries of the mind, and the wisdom that understands more clearly the process and the escape from temptation. It is expressed most characteristically by the gift of tears—at first bitter tears of sorrow, but ultimately tears of joy at the experience of God's overwhelmingly resourceful love. Second, purity is "a heart that shows mercy to all created nature," that sees into the essence of things, their inner being, and rejoices that all things were and are created good, and that the image of God remains imprinted on every human soul. Finally, perfection is described by Isaac as "profound humility"—the letting go of self, the self-emptying as demonstrated by the Christ who relinquishes even his grip on divinity, being found in human form (see Phil 2:5-11).

Then, having given away "the secrets of the Kingdom" in this brief survey, Isaac clarifies the purity of a merciful heart in words that have become emblematic of his whole spiritual teaching:

> 'And what is a merciful heart?' 'It is the heart's burning for the sake of the entire creation, for people, for birds, for animals, for demons, and for every created thing; and at the recollection and sight of them, the eyes of the merciful pour forth abundant tears. From the strong and vehement mercy that grips their heart and from their great compassion, their heart is humbled and they cannot bear to hear or to see any injury or slight sorrow in creation. For this reason they offer up prayers with tears continually even for irrational beasts, for the enemies of the truth, and for those who harm them, that they be protected and receive mercy.

> And in like manner they even pray for the reptiles, because of the great compassion that burns without measure in their heart in the likeness of God.'[8]

"Lord Jesus Christ, Son of God, have mercy on me," runs the Jesus Prayer. Those two words, "have mercy," stand for a radical shift in our being with God, with others and with ourselves. How far do our prayers and good wishes extend? How far do I travel into the mystery of others and of God? Isaac is gloriously inclusive in the passage: he includes all sentient beings in his prayers. Even the demons have their share in God's abundant mercy, as do the animals, the reptiles and the whole of creation.

The luminosity of the pure heart

Like Maximus the Confessor and Symeon the New Theologian, and indeed so many writers in this hesychastic tradition, purity of heart is associated by Isaac with a luminosity of spirit. This is a radiance that is hinted at in the descriptions of Moses in the Old Testament, or in the Transfiguration of Jesus on Mount Tabor, and subsequently depicted in the painted nimbus or halo surrounding saintly figures in the icons of Christian art. This is a fruit of their inner integration, their integrity and union with the Lord:

> When meditation is united to prayer in its luminous state, then the words of the Lord will fully apply, when he said, 'Where two or three are gathered together in my name, there am I among them' (Matt. 18.20). That is, the soul, body, and spirit; or the mind, meditation and prayer. And the three of them will end up in wonder . . . Once the mind's stirrings have begun to become luminous, then the heart is made humble and it becomes as though it is resident in some depth and as a result of this humbleness it approaches luminosity.[9]

How characteristic it is for Isaac, a born solitary, to interpret the "two or three gathered" as referring to "soul, body and spirit," or "the mind, meditation and prayer" rather than three eager disciples! Returning, again, to his threefold categorization of the spiritual path, Isaac integrates the experience of luminosity into the final stage of perfection:

> The end of repentance is the beginning of purity; the end of purity is the beginning of luminosity. The path of purity consists of labours of virtue, but for a person to be made luminous, this is the work of revelations. Purity is the stripping off of the passions; luminosity is the stripping off of suppositions and changes of mind, resulting in a precise knowledge of the mysteries.[10]

The ultimate state of "perfection" is now designated simply as "luminosity," transfiguration in light, becoming radiant with the diffusive goodness of God and God's compassion for all. It requires first a degree of stability in the mind, and results in "a precise knowledge of the mysteries." Again, this is a reference back to Evagrius with his threefold classification of dispassion (*apatheia*), forming the foundation for love (*agape*), leading to knowledge (*gnosis*). But don't wait for purity of heart before even beginning to pray, says Isaac, or you will never get started:

> You should not wait until you are purified from distraction of thoughts and only then have a desire to pray: rather, it is as a result of constancy of prayer and much toil over this that distraction will be dispersed from the mind. Whereas, if you wait until you see the mind completely raised up above all recollection of this world and only then begin on prayer, you will not ever pray![11]

Prayer is the way, not the destination, but one must travel the journey along the way of constancy in prayer before being able to arrive at the oasis of peace.

> I have said this, not wanting to give a hand to distraction or to give free license to the mind, or to show that the blow resulting from [distraction] is easy, but I am warning that we should not desist from prayer because of distraction. Nor should we cease

> from supplication on the grounds that we are not worthy, or that we are fine as we are . . . Therefore, with all these things, we strike out, and we pray, we are wounded, and we pray; we are innocent, and we pray; we are wallowing in guilt, and we pray; we are bespattered with the blood of our wounds, and we pray; we lie fallen, and we pray; the Lord gives us joy, and we pray; we are in the dark, and we pray; by all means, let us not cease from prayer on the grounds that we are not worthy, or are not in the right state for prayer. For our Lord said: 'The healthy do not need a doctor' (Matt. 9.12).[12]

God longs to be reconciled with us, and so we begin the return journey from our dissipation, knowing our unworthiness to be in God's presence, and all the while, like the prodigal son, rehearsing our speech which will be instantly forgotten as the loving arms of God enfold us and we find that we are already home.

Why God made the world

Isaac's emphasis of the transformation of the self in love echoes the great love with which God created the world:

> What profundity of richness, what mind and exalted wisdom is God's! What compassionate kindness and abundant goodness belongs to the Creator! With what purpose and with what love did He create this world and bring it into existence!
>
> . . .
>
> In love did he bring the world into existence; in love does he guide it during this its temporal existence; in love is he going to bring it to that wondrous transformed state, and in love will the world be swallowed up in the great mystery of him who has performed all these things; in love will the whole course of the governance of creation be finally comprised.[13]

This passage has echoes of the *Revelations of Divine Love* written by the English solitary and mystic Julian of Norwich (c. 1343–after

1416). In her final revelation she asks: What is the meaning in all this? To which the Lord replies that love was his meaning, only love, and nothing else would ever be able to sum up his meaning other than that one word, "love."

Isaac goes on to say that in God's design there is no distinction between the just and the wicked, no demarcation between those who may be more or less deserving of God's love. There is no first or last place in God's affections: all that is, seen and unseen, the whole of creation, is loved equally by God.

> And just as there is not a single nature who is in the first place or last place in creation in the Creator's knowledge—(I refer here to this knowledge) which was set in his purpose eternally, that he would bring them into being: it was not the case of his knowing one before or after another, but all of them equally without any before or after, in a twinkling of an eye—similarly there is no before or after in his love towards them: no greater or lesser amount (of love) is to be found with him at all. Therefore, just like the continual equality of his knowledge so too is the continual equality of his love; for he knew them (all) before they (ever) became just or sinners. Their Creator and his love did not change because they underwent change after he had brought them into being, nor does his purpose which exists eternally (change). And if it were otherwise, he would be subject to change just as created beings are—a shocking idea.[14]

The notion that God is unchangeable is one of the axioms of Christian theology: "For I the Lord do not change" (Mal 3:6); and "Jesus Christ is the same yesterday and today and for ever" (Heb 13:8), the beloved Son of "the Father of lights, with whom there is no variation or shadow due to change" (James 1:17). Therefore, if God loves the creation, then he has always loved it, and always will. If taken with utmost seriousness, this has profound effects on the doctrine of the incarnation and the redemption of humankind:

> If zeal were useful for the correction of fellow human beings, why did God the Word put on the body in order to turn the world

> towards his Father by means of kindness and in humble ways; why was he stretched out on the cross on behalf of sinners, handing over to suffering that holy body on behalf of the world? What I say is that God did this for no other reason apart from making known to the world the love he has, his purpose being so that through our greater love as a result of being aware of this, we might be captivated by his love. For the great power of the kingdom of heaven—which consists in love—will, through the death of his Son, provide the reason for the incarnation. It was not all the case that it was to deliver us from sins, nor was the death of our Lord for any other reason, apart alone for letting the world perceive the love that God has towards created beings.[15]

According to Isaac, the sole purpose of the incarnation was the demonstration of the love of God for the whole creation. God became human not so much to redeem fallen humanity but simply as a way to show humanity what it means to love. This is surely good news for Christians today. Many theologians have taught that the incarnation was an aspect of the atonement of God and humanity—that Jesus died for our sins, his coming among us being the result of the Fall. But Isaac says that Jesus died out of love for the world, not as a means of defeating the devil, or satisfying a wronged and angry God, or as a response to sin in any way, but simply out of the exuberance of love.

Isaac treats any ascription of anger to God as no more than a figurative way of speaking:

> Just because (the terms) wrath, anger, hatred, and the rest are used of the Creator, we should not imagine that he (actually) does anything in anger or hatred or zeal. Many figurative terms are employed in the Scriptures of God, terms which are far removed from his (true) nature.[16]

God does not hate anyone—his love is universal in its scope—and this has very specific effects on any doctrine of "the last things," that is, death, judgement, hell and heaven. God has ordained a mystery which we cannot yet understand; he has something up his sleeve, some plan that in his infinite creativity he will put into effect to cleanse and bring to perfection all living beings, including all humans and demons.[17] If God's activity is all grace, love, mercy and goodness, how can there be a preordained plan that allows for the payment of the penalty for sin? Mercy is the beginning and the end of all of God's actions on our behalf. To us it seems that God is responding to our predicament, our failure to love and worship him. But for God this is not a sequential process. This is not plan B, meant to rectify the disaster of the banishment from Eden and the descent into hell. Rather, this is plan A, what God always meant to be. There is no beginning to God's love, no moment when God set in motion his saving plan for the rescue of humanity. Creation is the moment of redemption, we were saved at the foundation of the world. And God's love is universal:

> He has a single ranking of complete and impassable love towards everyone, and he has a single caring concern for those who have fallen, just as much as for those who have not fallen. And it is clear that he does not abandon them the moment they fall, and that demons will not remain in their demonic state, and sinners (will not remain) in their sins; rather, he is going to bring them to a single equal state of perfection in relationship to his own Being—in a state in which the holy angels are now, in perfection of love and a passionless mind.[18]

All creatures will be raised to a better state than even that in which the angels exist now—"a single perfect state of knowledge," having one unified and enduring love, one will and purpose in life and death. For Isaac, even Gehenna, or the state of punishment for sin, is just a temporary state, necessary for some reason as yet hidden in the mind of God, but not in itself everlasting. Only love is everlasting; all else fades away and is forgotten, washed away by waves of joy:

> Where is that joy that all of a sudden is dispatched into the heart like waves, submerging all emotions? It grabs hold of the heart with an ineffable exultation, so that it almost seems to a person that he is raised up from the body, and is not standing on the

ground, all because of the heart's being seized by the waves of joy. Where is that insight that all of a sudden peeps out, silencing the tongue in wonder, rendering a person so that he has no recollection or thought, being sunk in the wonder that has fallen upon him as a result of no ordinary sensation, which the intellect receives from the verses [of the psalms]? Such a person becomes motionless in all his senses and his mind, these being deprived of all the things that bind up his soul with images and likenesses in prayer.[19]

Questions for reflection and discussion

- Of the many forms of prayer which do you find the most helpful?
- Which is more important—mercy or justice? Are they both necessary?
- Why did God make the world?

Further reading

A. M. Allchin (ed.), 1989, *Heart of Compassion: Daily Readings with St Isaac of Syria*, trans. Sebastian Brock, London: Darton, Longman & Todd.

Andrew D. Mayes, 2021, *Diving for Pearls: Exploring the Depths of Prayer with Isaac the Syrian*, Collegeville, MN: Liturgical Press.

Hilarion Alfeyev, 2000, *The Spiritual World of Isaac the Syrian*, Collegeville, MN: Cistercian Publications.

Notes

1 Andrew D. Mayes, 2021, *Diving for Pearls: Exploring the Depths of Prayer with Isaac the Syrian*, Collegeville, MN: Liturgical Press, pp. 9–10.

2 Quoted in Mayes, *Diving for Pearls*, p. 12.

3 Sebastian Brock, 1995, *Isaac of Nineveh (Isaac the Syrian), 'The Second Part,' Chapters IV–XLI*, Corpus Scriptorum Christianorum Orientalium vol. 555, Louvain: Peeters, p. 134.

4 Brock, *Isaac of Nineveh, the Second Part IV–XLI*, p. 143.

5 *The Ascetical Homilies of Saint Isaac the Syrian*, rev 2nd edn, 2011, trans. from the Greek and Syriac by the Holy Transfiguration Monastery, Boston, MA, p. 464.

6 Isaac, *Ascetical Homilies*, p. 465.

7 Isaac, *Ascetical Homilies*, p. 467.

8 Isaac, *Ascetical Homilies*, p. 491.

9 Sebastian Brock, 2022, *Saint Isaac of Nineveh: Headings on Spiritual Knowledge* (The Second Part, Chapters 1–3), Popular Patristics Series, trans. New York: St Vladimir's Seminary Press, p. 134.

10 Brock, *Headings*, p. 177.

11 Brock, *Headings*, p. 187.

12 Brock, *Headings*, p. 189.

13 Brock, *Isaac of Nineveh, the Second Part IV–XLI*, p. 160.

14 Brock, *Isaac of Nineveh, the Second Part IV–XLI*, p. 161.

15 Brock, *Headings*, pp. 211–12.

16 Brock, *Isaac of Nineveh, the Second Part IV–XLI*, p. 171.

17 See Brock, *Isaac of Nineveh, the Second Part IV–XLI*, p. 171.

18 Brock, *Isaac of Nineveh, the Second Part IV–XLI*, p. 175.

19 Brock, *Headings*, p. 122.

8

Symeon the New Theologian, Gregory Palamas and the Uncreated Light

One of the most celebrated authors of works exploring experiences of light is Saint Symeon the New Theologian (949–1022). Born into an aristocratic family, Symeon was able to join the higher echelons of government in Constantinople. At the age of 20 he first encountered a monk called Symeon Eulabes who became his spiritual director and confessor. A few years later a palace coup brought the political career of the younger Symeon to an end, and he became a monk at the monastery of St Mamas in Constantinople.

Symeon was a spiritually gifted man, having visions of his father in Christ being bathed in light and offering him protection from the perils of political and ecclesiastical life. He was given the epithet "New Theologian" to both differentiate him from and associate him with John the Evangelist, also known as John the Theologian, and the fourth-century bishop and spiritual writer, Gregory of Nazianzus, that is, Gregory the Theologian. However, his charismatic tendencies and the stern religious discipline he enforced at the monastery where he soon became abbot did not endear him to his fellow monks. He was drawn into public debates, as a result of which he was deposed and sent into exile. His legacy remains in the discourses he gave to his monks, full of the themes of repentance and the role of spiritual fatherhood, and the imagery of light and fire. Like many of the hesychasts, Symeon insisted on the importance of personally experiencing the divine light of Jesus Christ. It was only on such a basis that he approved of spiritual authority in the church, a policy which, if put into practice, would have rather drastically reduced the short-list of candidates for office! A typical example of the teaching of Symeon shows the vigor of his discourses and the sincerity with which he insists on the importance of a personal experience of the presence of Christ:

> He, however, who is united to God by faith and recognizes him by action is indeed enabled to see him by contemplation. He sees things of which I am not able to write. His mind sees strange visions and is wholly illuminated and becomes light, yet he is unable to conceive of them or describe them. His mind is itself light and sees all things as light, and the light has Life and imparts light to him who sees it. He sees himself wholly united to the light, and as he sees he concentrates on the vision and is as he was. He perceives the light in his soul and is in ecstasy. In his ecstasy he sees it from afar, but as he returns to himself he finds himself again in the midst of the light. He is thus altogether at a loss for words and concepts to describe what he has perceived in his vision.[1]

Symeon thus reflects on one of the great "I am . . ." sayings of the Fourth Gospel: "I am the light of the world. Whoever follows me will never walk in darkness but will have the light of life" (John 8:12). This self-reference by Jesus in the Gospel of John is the calling of Symeon also, that he might experience the light of Christ in his life too, in a way that passes understanding.

Although Symeon emphasizes the ineffability of such experiences, he did write down on a few occasions the experiences that became fundamental to his understanding of the way of salvation. In one of his discourses, speaking in the third person of a young man he calls "George," he is nonetheless plainly describing himself:

> One day, as he stood and recited, 'God, have mercy upon me, a sinner' (Luke 18.13), uttering it with his mind rather than his mouth, suddenly a flood of divine radiance appeared from above and filled all the room. As this happened the young man lost all awareness of his surroundings and forgot that he was in a house or that he was under a roof. He saw nothing but light all around him and did not know if he was standing on the ground. He was not afraid of falling; he was not concerned with the world, nor

> did anything pertaining to men and corporeal beings enter into his mind. Instead, he was wholly in the presence of immaterial light and seemed to himself to have turned into light. Oblivious of all the world he was filled with tears and with ineffable joy and gladness. His mind then ascended to heaven and beheld yet another light, which was clearer than that which was close at hand. In a wonderful manner there appeared to him, standing close to that light, the saint of whom we have spoken, the old man equal to angels, who had given him the commandment and the book.[2]

This experience of light happens while the young man is reciting the prayer of the tax-collector in the temple, as described in a parable of Jesus (Luke 18:9-14). This is one of the New Testament prayers that form the background to the Jesus Prayer itself, showing how Symeon places himself as a link in the chain of this tradition. The "old man equal to angels" is a reference to Symeon's spiritual father Eulabes, fulfilling the gospel precept of becoming like an angel in this very life (see Luke 20:34-36). "The commandment and the book" refer to a text on prayer by Mark the Ascetic, and the instruction of how to pray passed on by his spiritual guide. And so Symeon takes up the baton of the hesychasts for another generation, and encourages his fellow monks to do the same.

Hymns of love

Although much of his theological writing comes in the form of discourses, Symeon also composed numerous hymns, as a way of trying to reconcile the theology of the church with his own vivid experiences of union with God:

Hymn 15

You are unmoved, yet ever-moving,
and you are wholly outside of creation,
   wholly in every creature.
The whole of you fills all things,
   yet you are wholly outside of everything,

above all things, Master, above all beginning . . .
For you are not a thing among all beings,
  but you are superior to everything;
for you are the cause of all beings
  as the Creator of all things,
and on this account you are apart from everything,
so high beyond the perception of any being.[3]

Beyond being and non-being—these are descriptions of God that go back to the *Mystical Theology* by Dionysius the Areopagite in the sixth century, most probably writing in a monastery somewhere in Syria. Dionysius attempts to explore the limits of theological language, and here Symeon picks up the mantle of one who loves beyond reason, and who prays that he might go beyond all words into the resonant silence of unknowing. Even to say that "God is" is already too great a concession to human language; but to say that "God is not" is even further from the truth. God is within, and yet also "without," in all senses of that word—"outside" as well as having nothing by which we could grasp God's self. God is the disorientation of the human mind, the loss of boundaries, the silence of concepts, as well as the final, whole, blissful reunion with that which can only be known as love.

Some of Symeon's most startling teachings come in the form of love songs, full of desire (*ἔρως/eros*) for God, expressed by piling on layer after layer of paradox:

Hymn 30

I was amazed, I was astonished,
I was frightened, and I rejoiced,
and understood the wonder,
how he is outside everything,
while I am within everything.
Alone I see him seeing me,
I do not discern where he is,
how great he is, or what nature,
or what kind, or whom I see,
or how I see, or what I see.

Yet seeing what I have seen,
and wailing because I cannot
know this manner,
nor understand fully,
nor can I perceive just a bit,
how the one whom I see sees me.
Again I saw him within
my house and within my earthen jar
where suddenly he became whole,
ineffably united to me,
unspeakably joined,
and mixed in me without mixing,
like the fire in the iron itself,
and the light in the crystal,
and he made me like a fire,
and made me like light,
and I became that
which I had seen before
and had contemplated from afar,
and I do not know how to explain to you
the paradox of this manner,
for I was not able to know,
nor do I know now by any means,
how he entered, how he was united.[4]

Language such as this has parallels with the Song of Songs in the Old Testament, the love song that has become an allegory for the longing of the soul for God, and the love of Christ for his church. In the Song the soul longs to see and be seen by her beloved, and searches for him everywhere, but is disconsolate when she cannot find the one whom she loves. The mutual gaze of love is the means of salvation, a theme typified in the icons of the Holy Trinity, or of the Madonna and child, the one full of grace gazing out of the icon and drawing the worshipper into this sacred relationship of mercy and love.

Symeon speaks of this experience primarily with the metaphor of light—the light that is at first far off, but then is comingled with his own being, like an iron bar glowing red hot in a fire, or like a crystal refracting light. And yet this presence of God is found in the earthen jar of the body, as Paul says in the Second Letter to the Corinthians: "But we have this treasure in clay jars, so that it may be made clear that this extraordinary power belongs to God and does not come from us" (2 Cor 4:7).

Paradoxically, for Symeon, it is dispassion that brings the soul closest to her beloved:

Hymn 46

The dispassion produced in me is the unutterable
  pleasure of communion,
and boundless desire for the wedding feast,
  for union full of God,
partaking of which I also became dispassionate,
I was burned up with pleasure,
  blazing with desire for it,
and I shared in the light, yes, and I became light,
higher than all passion, outside all wickedness.
For passion does not touch the light of dispassion,
just as the shadow or darkness of night
  cannot touch the sun.[5]

This passionate dispassion is the boundless desire for God, the fire that burns up the one who loves beyond reason and explanation. All that is left is the fire of love, the light which blazes in her heart, and draws the soul to be lost forever in the fire of the living God. In his darkness, Symeon reaches out to God, just to touch his hand, not languorously like Adam offering a forefinger on the ceiling of Michaelangelo's Sistine Chapel, but passionately like Mary Magdalene reaching out to Jesus in the garden of the resurrection, as portrayed in Titian's *Noli Me Tangere*.

Hymn 50

O Absolute Monarch,
  who alone are supremely compassionate,
I thank you from all my heart,

because you did not look away when I lay below
in darkness, but you touched me
  with your divine hand.
When I saw her, at once I got up rejoicing.
For she shone brighter than the sun.
I, the wretch, strove to seize your hand,
and immediately she vanished from my eyes,
and again I was entirely in darkness.
I fell to the floor mourning and weeping,
rolling about and groaning vehemently,
yearning to see again your divine hand.
You reached out, she was seen more clearly by me,
and embracing her I kissed her.
Oh kindness and abundant compassion,
the creator has given his hand to be kissed,
the hand that sustains the universe with her strength,
oh gift, oh inexpressible present![6]

The hand of God is given a feminine pronoun here as it would have in the original Greek. Symeon reaches out to her (the hand of God) as a drowning man in a torrential river desperate to reach out and be saved. Symeon's hymn is in the language of love songs, the whisperings of desire rather than the declarations of a creed. There is a beauty in such language, an enjoyment of the relationship with God that can be heard most often in Pentecostal churches today. Symeon would perhaps feel more at home in a modern charismatic service of praise, rather than in the measured devotion of Matins from the Book of Common Prayer.

Finally, Symeon reels off his love in a string of epithets for God, in a kind of litany of love:

Hymn 58

You know that I have you alone
as my life, and word, and knowledge, and wisdom,
Saviour God, and patron in life,
And life's breath of my humble soul.
I am a stranger and humble in words.

You are my hope, you are my support,
You are my shelter, you my refuge,
You my boast, my wealth, my glory.
You, Logos, according to your compassion,
wanted to receive me from the world, me the stranger,
the unworthy, the one more worthless than
every human being, worse than every irrational beast.
And because of this I take confidence in your mercy,
and I beg of you, and I babble, and prostrate myself.[7]

The language at the end is almost too much. And yet the poet is in good company with Anselm of Canterbury (c. 1033–1109), who wrote highly emotive prayers addressed to Jesus and the saints, and with Francis of Assisi (1192–1226), another poet and lover of God, who also composed Praises of God, and who overflowed with devotion in all the prayers he composed for his letters and the *Earlier Rule*.

St Gregory Palamas

Although we have been talking about the hesychastic tradition throughout the first millennium of Christian spirituality, it is only in the fourteenth century that this way of praying received its archetypal definition. Chief among those leading this hesychastic renewal was Gregory Palamas (1296–1359), a monk of Mount Athos in Greece and later Archbishop of Thessalonica. Gregory was born in Constantinople, receiving an extensive education, all the while feeling called to enter the religious life, which he recommended to his brothers and sisters and their widowed mother. When he was 22 years of age he entered a monastery on Mount Athos, a peninsula in northern Greece isolated from the mainland and populated solely by monks since the tenth century. There he devoted himself to the monastic life in seclusion from all secular affairs. With the encroachment of the Turks Gregory had to leave Athos and settled in the Greek city of Thessalonica for the next 15 years, where he was ordained priest.

Eventually Gregory was able to return to Athos, to renew his contemplative vocation. But other matters intervened. He became involved in a dispute with a Greek monk named Barlaam, from Calabria in Italy, concerning the validity of hesychastic prayer. Barlaam strongly advocated a purely rational approach to Christian practice, criticizing the practice of contemplative prayer as lived and taught on Mount Athos. He stressed the unknowability of God, in contrast to the belief among the hesychasts that they were able to see the uncreated light of Christ as a result of their prayer. Rising to the occasion, Gregory wrote *Triads in defence of the Holy Hesychasts* (c. 1338), which became the definitive statement of hesychasm for centuries to come. Gregory's views were accepted as orthodox by three fourteenth-century synods, which collectively became known as the Ninth Ecumenical Council. In 1347 Gregory was consecrated Archbishop of Thessalonica, though hampered in taking up his responsibilities by the turbulent political situation which included his imprisonment by the Turks for a year, having been arrested when on a voyage to Constantinople.

The crux of Gregory's view was that the hesychasts did indeed have direct personal experience of the energies (*ενέργειαι/energeiai*) of God, knowing what God does, even if the essence (*οὐσία/ousia*) of God was hidden, not knowing what God is in God's self. According to Gregory, the energies of God are revealed in the vision of the uncreated light of Christ, visible to the disciples Peter, James and John at the transfiguration of Christ on Mount Tabor. This same light could be experienced in the dynamic stillness bestowed by God and facilitated by repentance and contemplative practice, and especially by the recitation of the Jesus Prayer.

In this practice of prayer, Gregory encourages the use of the breath, even for beginners:

> It is not out of place to teach people, especially beginners, that they should look at themselves, and introduce their own mind within themselves through control of breathing. A prudent man will not forbid someone who does not as yet contemplate himself to use certain methods to recall his mind within himself, for those newly approaching this struggle find that their mind, when recollected, continually becomes dispersed again. It is thus necessary for such people constantly to bring it back once more; but

> in their inexperience, they fail to grasp that nothing in the world is in fact more difficult to contemplate and more mobile and shifting than the mind.[8]

The mind is constantly on the move and needs help to find a more restful and alert state. Watching the breath, without strain or stress, is helpful in the gentle stabilizing of the mind, and is part of what John Climacus taught back in the seventh century when he recommended that the monk should keep the mind within the body, not letting it wander off from the point of focus.

> This is why certain masters recommend them to control the movement inwards and outwards of the breath, and to hold it back a little; in this way, they will also be able to control the mind together with the breath—this, at any rate, until such time as they have made progress, with the aid of God, have restrained the intellect from becoming distracted by what surrounds it, have purified it and truly become capable of leading it to a 'unified recollection'. One can state that this recollection is a spontaneous effect of the attention of the mind, for the to-and-fro movement of the breath becomes quietened during intensive reflection, especially with those who maintain inner quiet in body and soul.[9]

Like Maximus the Confessor, Gregory Palamas sees the body and the passions of the mind not as enemies to be destroyed or denied, but as co-workers in the process of divinization, friends by whose strength and encouragement one is able to complete the course. Here we find our old friend dispassion (or "impassibility") directing all things well:

> Impassibility does not consist in mortifying the passionate part of the soul, but in removing it from evil to good, and directing its energies towards divine things . . . and the impassible man is one who no longer possesses any evil disposition, but is rich in good ones, who is marked by the virtues . . . For it is the misuse of the powers of the soul which engenders the terrible passions, just as misuse of the knowledge of created things en-

> genders the 'wisdom which has become folly' (1 Cor. 1.20). But if one uses these things properly, then through the knowledge of created things, spiritually understood, one will arrive at knowledge of God; and through the passionate part of the soul which has been orientated towards the end for which God created it, one will practise the corresponding virtues.[10]

The passions, rightly employed, provide the momentum necessary to turn oneself around and face the direction of the light of Christ, ready to arrive at the knowledge of God. Body and soul cooperate together in this journey, supplying the necessary strength and harmony to rest in uninterrupted remembrance of God. In this practice, gentleness towards others is more helpful than rebuke, as it is a reflection of the gentleness of God in his mercy towards us:

> Our eyes must acquire a gentle glance, attractive to others, and conveying the mercy from on high (for it is written, 'He who has a gentle look will receive grace'—Prov. 12.13a LXX). Similarly, our ears must be attentive to the divine instructions, not only to hear them, but (as David says) 'to remember the commandments of God . . . in order to perform them' (Ps. 103.18) . . . Our tongues, our hands and feet must likewise be at the service of the Divine Will. Is not such a practice of the commandments of God a common activity of body and soul, and how can such activity darken and blind the soul?[11]

Too often, a severe rejection of the body has marred the description of the spiritual path, based on an overly platonic separation of body and soul, with the concomitant rejection or repression of the body. This has overflowed into a rejection of the insights of women, seen as representative of the physical nature, rather than the supposed spiritual nature of men. Gregory, monk though he is and writing on a mountain separated from women, still clearly teaches the harmony of body and soul. The *nous*, the enlightened mind common to all women and men, brings the whole of creation to participate in the transfiguring light of Christ, such that all created beings are made one and divinized in God.

Questions for reflection and discussion

- Is the language of desire appropriate in our relationship with God?
- Have you used awareness of the breath in your prayers? Does it help?
- Do you know of people who seem to radiate light and peace?

Further reading

Hannah Hunt, 2015, *A Guide to St. Symeon the New Theologian*, Eugene, OR: Cascade Books.

C. J. deCatanzaro (trans.), 1980, *Saint Symeon the New Theologian: The Discourses*, Classics of Western Spirituality, New York: Paulist Press.

John Meyendorff (ed.) and Nicholas Gendle (trans.), 1983, *Gregory Palamas—The Triads*, Classics of Western Spirituality, New Jersey: Paulist Press.

Notes

1 C. J. deCatanzaro (trans.), 1980, *Saint Symeon the New Theologian: The Discourses*, Classics of Western Spirituality, New York: Paulist Press, p. 56.

2 deCatanzaro, *Symeon the New Theologian*, pp. 245–6.

3 Daniel K. Griggs, 2010, *Divine Eros: Hymns of Saint Symeon the New Theologian*, New York: St Vladimir's Seminary Press, p. 84.

4 Griggs, *Divine Eros*, pp. 242–3.

5 Griggs, *Divine Eros*, p. 335.

6 Griggs, *Divine Eros*, p. 352.

7 Griggs, *Divine Eros*, p. 398.

8 John Meyendorff (ed.) and Nicholas Gendle (trans.), 1983, *Gregory Palamas—The Triads*, Classics of Western Spirituality, New Jersey: Paulist Press, p. 45.

9 Meyendorff, *The Triads*, p. 46.

10 Meyendorff, *The Triads*, p. 54.

11 Meyendorff, *The Triads*, p. 55.

Postscript

St Porphyrios and the Silence of Joy

And so, we have almost come to the end of our journey in the company of the men and women of the hesychastic tradition. We began with Antony and Arsenius leading us into the silence of the desert, wrestling with demons and weeping for their sins and out of compassion for the world. There we defined some of the more technical terms that surface again and again in this tradition: such as silence, dispassion, mind and heart. Then, Evagrius took us by the hand and led us through his own understanding of the passions, as he talked back at the forces of darkness, and found meaning and coherence in the classification of the thoughts against which he struggled again and again. Then Syncletica and the desert mothers brought their distinctive brand of wisdom to the table and the discussion, speaking their truth without fear.

Moving on, we heard from the two Macarii—the teacher of Evagrius, and the author of the Macarian Homilies, with Diadochus skilfully interweaving the strands of the hesychast tradition beginning to form in heart and mind, and introducing us to monologistic prayer, and the practice of calling out to the Lord Jesus for help. Then followed Mark the Ascetic and John Climacus, guiding us in the ascent of Mount Sinai, explaining along the way about the sequences of thought in the process of temptation, and how to break free from these circles of distress. Next came the Old Men of Gaza, and Hesychius, going much further into the practicalities of prayer and how to balance watchfulness, attentiveness and the Jesus Prayer itself. Maximus the Confessor took us back to some of the inspirations of Evagrius, and mellowed them with 400 texts on love. Isaac of Syria proved himself a lover of silence, and acted as a wise pilot to bring to a safe haven souls lost in the oceans of God's love.

Finally, Symeon the New Theologian and Gregory Palamas fleshed out the form of the hesychast tradition as it has come down to us today, giving both theological affirmation and practical inspiration to those who find God leading them in such ways of prayer.

This is a living tradition of prayer, handed on from one generation to another, one elder to his or her disciple. At times it has been well-known, even infamous; at other times almost lost in obscurity. Thankfully there is currently something of a revival, and a broadening out of the range of people finding meaning and encouragement in this way of prayer. Contemporary teachers, well known in Greece for their wisdom and compassion, include the recent saints Paisios and Porphyrios. May they guide us further, and may all those who have been helped by this practice find the Lord whom they seek, who will suddenly come to the temple of their heart, and sit on the throne of mercy, full of grace and truth.

St Porphyrios and the silence of joy

Among the most widely loved hesychasts of recent times, Saint Porphyrios (1906–1991) stands out as a shining example of devotion to God, and of kindness and humility in his relationships with others. Born into a poor family with little formal education, Porphyrios spent his earliest years tending a flock of sheep in the hills above his home village. At the age of seven he was sent by his mother to work in a hardware store where his hard-working conscientious nature made a deep impression on those who knew him. After two years he went to work in a grocer's shop run by a relative, where a chance encounter with two monks ignited in him a vocation to the monastic life. Twice he ran away, trying to get to the Holy Mountain of Athos, with little or no money in his pocket. Each time he abandoned his journey and returned home, unable to bear the prospect of separation from his family. The third time he succeeded in reaching Athos on the ferry boat from the mainland and disembarked, not knowing where he would go next. Seeing him there at a loss as to what to do, an old monk befriended him and, unable to persuade him to return home, effectively smuggled him into the monastic republic. Athos being a place where women and "beardless youths" cannot go, the monk pretended that the young boy was his orphaned nephew, with no one else to care for him. For the next several years Porphyrios stayed at the hermitage where this monk lived with a single companion, the young boy gradually becoming familiar with the patterns of monastic life. There he learned how to read the Psalms and the Gospels, committing much of them to memory, and was taught the skill of hand-carving pieces of wood into small devotional scenes. Everything was done under obedience, as is the style of life on Athos; nothing was done without the command or permission of the elders. All of this is done in order to stand back from personal inclination, being willing to let go of self and learn the pattern of life as it has been lived for centuries.

As soon as he was able, Porphyrios was clothed as a novice monk, and gladly lived a life of great simplicity, working in the garden at the hermitage, and running errands all around the peninsula. While still a teenager, he received the monastic cassock, known as the "Great Schema," and was tonsured as a professed monk. He attended the worship at the nearby monastery as often as he could, and would immerse himself in the grandeur of the services, lost in the beauty of the icons and the scent of the incense. He would fast often and spend long hours in prayer, particularly the Jesus Prayer, as he ran his knotted woolen prayer-rope through his fingers.

Once in the early hours of the morning, while it was still dark, he went into the dim church building to quietly say his prayers. There he saw another monk enter, look around him to see if he was alone, and start to say the Jesus Prayer and call out to the Theotokos, Mary the Mother of God. As Porphyrios watched, hidden behind a pillar, the old monk (named Demas) went into a kind of trance, an ecstasy of prayer and devotion. The young monk was drawn irresistibly into the prayers of the elder, and began to shed warm tears of repentance and joy. Something about that experience changed him for ever. He was filled with the grace of God communicated by the elder, and from that moment was given the gift of clear sight, what is sometimes called discernment, or the ability to read souls.

In later years Porphyrios looked back on this time living with his beloved elders as a period of great consolation. Whenever he could he would run through the deserted areas of the mountain, seeking out solitary places to pray. Eventually his health broke down after overexerting himself on his errands, and he was unable to regain his strength on the somewhat meager rations of food available. With great reluctance he returned to his family, leaving behind what he regarded as an idyllic way of life. Returning to live with his mother and sister in a built-up area of Athens was nothing if not a shock to his system. Amid all the noise and bustle of city life he longed for the peace and quiet of the Holy Mountain.

When he was sufficiently recovered from his illness, he began looking for work and ended up being appointed as the chaplain to a hospital in Athens. There was a caravan in which he could sleep, and a chapel where he could celebrate the Holy Mysteries of the liturgy. At first, he thought he had made a terrible mistake: the neighborhood was so chaotic, and just opposite his chapel there was a vendor of music who blared out pop songs all day, drowning out any prayers and chants from the services Porphyrios held for staff and patients. After getting an earful of abuse, Porphyrios simply resolved to sing louder, and eventually managed to convert the shop owner to a more neighborly approach to business.

The hospital became his life. Sometimes people would come to the doctors and be "referred" to the chaplain to hold them in his prayers. Sometimes they would come directly to him and be sent on to the medical staff for the necessary treatment. With his simplicity of heart he could "diagnose" spiritual sicknesses, and after studying medical textbooks was able to suggest to the medics what might be the physical problem. Some visitors would come for spiritual direction or to confess their sins; in some cases he would tell them their sins or their symptoms before they had even opened their mouth. He seemed to instinctively know the whole situations of family strife before even being introduced, though he made little of it and just offered solid advice on how to live the married life as much as possible without stress, and how to raise children to become pillars of church and society.

In all that he did, Porphyrios would be constantly praying and calling on the Lord Jesus Christ, thus embodying the hesychastic tradition. His teachings were based wholly on the love of God and the attitude of gratefulness, despite the many ailments that plagued him as he got older.

Words of life

In his talks and counsels, Porphyrios reveals a soul in love with God in the person of Jesus Christ, saying that this relationship with Christ begins before the foundation of the world:

> The three persons of the Holy Trinity constitute the eternal Church. The angels and human beings existed in the thought and love of the Triune God from the beginning. We human beings were not born now, we existed before the ages in God's omniscience . . . Christ united the body of the Church with heaven and with earth: with angels, men and all created things, with all of God's creation—with the animals and birds, with each tiny wild flower and each microscopic insect. The Church thus became the fullness of him who fills all in all (Eph. 1.23), that is, of Christ. Everything is in Christ and with Christ. This is the mystery of the Church.[1]

This mystery of the Church is Christ, revealed in the unity of the Church; and believers are incomplete without each other, sharing each other's joy and pain:

> The important thing is for us to enter into the Church—to unite ourselves with our fellow men, with the joys and sorrows of each and every one, to feel that they are our own, to pray for everyone, to have care for their salvation, to forget about ourselves, to do everything for them just as Christ did for us. In the Church we become one with each unfortunate, suffering and sinful soul. No one should wish to be saved alone without all others being saved. It is a mistake for someone to pray for himself, that he himself may be saved. We must love one another and pray that no soul be lost, that all may enter into the Church. That is what counts.[2]

It is with this attitude that one should enter monastic life, he would say, if that is God's particular gift to us. But in all walks of life, the keynote should be joy, the kind of joy that transforms with a holy intoxication of love.

> Christ is joy, the true light, happiness. Christ is our hope. Our relation to Christ is love, *eros*, passion, enthusiasm, longing for the divine. Christ is everything. He is our love. He is the object of our desire. This passionate longing for Christ is a love that cannot be taken away. This is where joy flows from . . . Fast as much as you can, make as many prostrations as you can, attend as many vigils as you like, but be joyful. Have Christ's joy. It is the joy that lasts forever, that brings eternal happiness. It is the joy of our Lord that gives assured serenity, serene delight and full happiness. All-joyful joy that surpasses every joy. Christ desires and delights in scattering joy, in enriching his faithful with joy. I pray that your joy may be full (John 16.24). This is what our religion is. This is the direction we must take. Christ is Paradise, my children. What is Paradise? It is Christ. Paradise begins here and now.[3]

The key to the spiritual life is the grace-filled practice of the Jesus Prayer, prayed with open arms, actively waiting for the Savior to be revealed in one's own heart, and in all people. If someone thinks that they are beginning to make progress or have already arrived at the prayer of the heart, then that is an indication that they have further to go. The mind should be kept focused and still, picturing nothing in the mind, forming no images, just gently repeating the phrase, "Lord Jesus Christ, have mercy on me." Then they can see how far that "me" can stretch, so that it encompasses all people, all of creation. Sometimes it is good to say the prayer, "Lord Jesus Christ, have mercy on me," out loud so that you hear it with your ears. We are body and soul and there is interaction between the two. But when you have fallen in love with Christ you prefer silence and spiritual prayer. Then words cease. It is inner silence that precedes, accompanies and follows the divine visitation, the divine union and co-mingling of the soul with the divine. When you find yourself in this state, words are not needed. This is something you experience, something that cannot be explained. Only the person who experiences this stage understands it. The sense of love floods through you and unites you with Christ. You are filled with joy and exultation which shows that you have the divine, perfect love within you. Divine love is selfless, simple and pure. The most perfect form of prayer is silent prayer. Silence. "Let all mortal flesh keep silence." Amid the mystery of silence assimilation to God takes place.[4]

Question for reflection and discussion

- Who are your favorite saints?

Further reading

Kyriacos C. Markides, 2001, *The Mountain of Silence: A Search for Orthodox Spirituality*, New York: Image/Doubleday.

Fr Constantine (Charles) J. Simones, 2013, *Miraculous Occurrences and Counsels of Elder Porphyrios*, Milessi: The Transfiguration of the Saviour Publications.

Hieromonk Isaac, 2016, *Saint Paisios of Mount Athos*, 2nd edn, trans. Hieromonk Alexis (Trader) and Fr Peter Heers, Chalkidiki, Greece: Holy Monastery 'Saint Arsenios the Cappadocian.'

Notes

1 Porphyrios, 2005, *Wounded by Love: The Life and the Wisdom of Saint Prophyrios*, edited from an archive of notes and recordings by the Sisters of the Holy Convent of Chrysopigi, Greece, Limni, Evia: Denise Harvey (publisher), p. 88.

2 Porphyrios, *Wounded*, pp. 88–9.

3 Porphyrios, *Wounded*, p. 96.

4 Porphyrios, *Wounded*, p. 127.

Bibliography

Agapios, Monk, 2013, *The Divine Flame Elder Porphyrios Lit in My Heart*, 2nd edn, Milessi: The Transfiguration of the Savior Publications.

Alfeyev, Hilarion, 2000, *The Spiritual World of Isaac the Syrian*, Collegeville, MN: Cistercian Publications.

——— (ed.), 2015, *St Isaac the Syrian and His Spiritual Legacy*, New York: St Vladimir's Seminary Press.

Allchin, A. M. (ed.), 1989, *Heart of Compassion: Daily Readings with St Isaac of Syria*, trans. Sebastian Brock, London: Darton, Longman & Todd.

Allen, Pauline and Bronwen Neil (eds), 2015, *The Oxford Handbook of Maximus the Confessor*, Oxford: Oxford University Press.

Amis, Robin, 2002, *Holy Hesychia: The Stillness that Knows God—In Defence of the Holy Hesychasts, Book One, Saint Gregory Palamas*, Wells: Pleroma Publishing.

Balthasar, Hans Urs von, 2003, *Cosmic Liturgy: The Universe According to Maximus the Confessor*, San Francisco, CA: Ignatius Press.

Bamberger John Eudes OCSO, 1981, *Evagrius Ponticus: The Praktikos & Chapters on Prayer*, Collegeville, MN: Cistercian Publications.

Barrington-Ward, Simon, 1996, *The Jesus Prayer*, Oxford: The Bible Reading Fellowship.

Bathrellos, Demetrios, 2015, 'Passions, Ascesis, and the Virtues' in Pauline Allen and Bronwen Neil, *The Oxford Handbook of Maximus the Confessor*, Oxford: Oxford University Press, pp. 287–306.

Berthold, George C., 1985, *Maximus Confessor—Selected Writings*, Classics of Western Spirituality, London: SPCK.

Bingaman, Brock and Bradley Nassif (eds), 2012, *The Philokalia: A Classic Text of Orthodox Spirituality*, Oxford: Oxford University Press.

Brakke, David, 2009, *Evagrius of Pontus: Talking Back (Antirrhetikos), a Monastic Handbook for Combating Demons*, Collegeville, MN: Cistercian Publications.

Brock, Sebastian, 1985, *The Luminous Eye: the Spiritual World Vision of Saint Ephrem*, Collegeville, MN: Cistercian Publications.

———, 1987, *The Syriac Fathers on Prayer and the Spiritual Life*, Collegeville, MN: Cistercian Publications.

———, 1995, *Isaac of Nineveh (Isaac the Syrian), 'The Second Part,' Chapters IV–XLI*, Corpus Scriptorum Christianorum Orientalium vol. 555, Louvain: Peeters.

———, 2022, *Saint Isaac of Nineveh: Headings on Spiritual Knowledge (The Second Part, Chapters 1–3)*, Popular Patristics Series, New York: St Vladimir's Seminary Press.

Bunge, Gabriel, 2002, *Earthen Vessels: The Practice of Personal Prayer According to the Patristic Tradition*, San Francisco, CA: Ignatius Press.

———, 2009, *Dragon's Wine and Angel's Bread: The Teaching of Evagrius Ponticus on Anger and Meekness*, New York: St Vladimir's Seminary Press.

Casiday, A. M., 2006, *Evagrius Ponticus*, London: Routledge.

Cherubim, Archimandrite (Karambelas), 2000, *Contemporary Ascetics of Mount Athos*, volume 1, Platina, CA: St Hermon of Alaska Brotherhood.

Chryssavgis, John, 2003, *In the Heart of the Desert: The Spirituality of the Desert Fathers and Mothers*, Bloomington, IN: World Wisdom.

———, 2003, *Letters from the Desert—Barsanuphius and John, A Selection of Questions and Responses*, Popular Patristics Series, New York: St Vladimir's Seminary Press.

———, 2004, *John Climacus: From the Egyptian Desert to the Sinaite Mountain*, Aldershot: Ashgate.

———, 2004, *Light Through Darkness: The Orthodox Tradition*, Traditions of Christian Spirituality Series, London: Darton, Longman & Todd.

———, 2002, with Pachomios Penkett, *Abba Isaiah of Scetis: Ascetic Discourses*, Collegeville, MN: Cistercian Publications.

———, 2013, with Bruce V. Foltz (eds), *Toward an Ecology of Transfiguration: Orthodox Christian Perspectives on Environment, Nature, and Creation*, New York: Fordham University Press.

———, 2022, *The Letters of Barsanuphius and John: Desert Wisdom for Everyday Life*, London: T&T Clark.

Cook, Christopher C. H., 2011, *The Philokalia and the Inner Life: On Passions and Prayer*, Cambridge: James Clarke & Co.

Cooper, Adam G., 2005, *The Body in St Maximus the Confessor: Holy Flesh, Wholly Deified*, Oxford Early Christian Studies, Oxford: Oxford University Press.

Cutsinger, James S., 2002 (ed.), *Paths to the Heart: Sufism and the Christian East*, Bloomington, IN: World Wisdom.

Dalrymple, William, 1997, *From The Holy Mountain: A Journey in the Shadow of Byzantium*, London: HarperCollins.

deCatanzaro, C. J., 1980, *Symeon the New Theologian: The Discourses*, Classics of Western Spirituality, New York: Paulist Press.

Dysinger, Luke, OSB, 2005, *Psalmody and Prayer in the Writings of Evagrius Ponticus*, Oxford: Oxford University Press.

Ermatinger, Cliff, 2010, *Following the Footsteps of the Invisible: The Complete Works of Diadochus of Photikē*, Collegeville, MN: Liturgical Press.

Gillett, Lev (A monk of the Orthodox Church), 1987, 2nd edn, *The Jesus Prayer*, New York: St Vladimir's Seminary Press.

Griggs, Daniel K., 2010, *Divine Eros: Hymns of Saint Symeon the New Theologian*, Popular Patristics Series, New York: St Vladimir's Seminary Press.

Gross, Jules, 2002, *The Divinization of the Christian: According to the Greek Fathers*, Anaheim, CA: A&C Press.

Harmless, William SJ, 2004, *Desert Christians: An Introduction to the Literature of Early Monasticism*, Oxford: Oxford University Press.

Hausherr, Irénée, SJ, 1978, *The Name of Jesus*, trans. Charles Cummings OCSO, Collegeville, MN: Cistercian Publications.

———, 1982, *Penthos: The Doctrine of Compunction in the Christian East*, Collegeville, MN: Cistercian Publications.

Hierotheos, Metropolitan of Nafpaktos, 1991, 3rd edn, *A Night in the Desert of the Holy Mountain: Discussion with a Hermit on the Jesus Prayer*, trans. Effie Mavromichali, Levadia: Birth of the Theotokos Monastery.

Hopkins, Gerard Manley, 1970, *The Poems of Gerard Manley Hopkins*, 4th edn, W. H. Gardner and N. H. MacKenzie (eds), Oxford: Oxford University Press.

Hunt, Hannah, 2015, *A Guide to St. Symeon the New Theologian*, Eugene, OR: Cascade Books.

Isaac, Hieromonk, 1998, *Isaac of Nineveh: On Ascetical Life*, trans. Mary Hansbury, New York: St Vladimir's Seminary Press.

———, *The Ascetical Homilies of Saint Isaac the Syrian*, revd 2nd edn, 2011, translated from the Greek and Syriac by the Holy Transfiguration Monastery, Boston, MA.

———, 2016, *Isaac the Syrian's Spiritual Works*, Piscataway, NJ: Georgias Press.

———, 2016, *Saint Paisios of Mount Athos*, 2nd edn, trans. Hieromonk Alexis (Trader) and Fr Peter Heers, Chalkidiki, Greece: Holy Monastery 'Saint Arsenios the Cappadocian.'

Johnson, Christopher D. L., 2010, *The Globalization of Hesychasm and the Jesus Prayer: Contesting Contemplation*, London: Continuum.

Jones, Cheslyn, Geoffrey Wainright and Edward Yarnold SJ (eds), 1986, *The Study of Spirituality*, London: SPCK.

[Joseph the Hesychast], 1998, *Monastic Wisdom: The Letters of Elder Joseph the Hesychast*, Florence, AZ: St. Anthony's Greek Orthodox Monastery.

———, 1999, *Elder Joseph the Hesychast: Struggles—Experiences—Teachings (1898–1959)*, trans. Elizabeth Theokritoff, Mount Athos: Monastery of Vatopaidi.

Kadloubovsky, E., and G. E. H. Palmer, 1951, *Writings from the Philokalia on Prayer of the Heart*, London: Faber and Faber.

Konstantinovsky, Julia, 2016, *Evagrius Ponticus: The Making of a Gnostic*, London: Routledge.

Laird, Martin, 2006, *Into the Silent Land: The Practice of Contemplation*, London: Darton, Longman & Todd.

———, 2011, *A Sunlit Absence: Silence, Awareness, and Contemplation*, Oxford: Oxford University Press.

———, 2019, *An Ocean of Light: Contemplation, Transformation, and Liberation*, Oxford: Oxford University Press.

Leloup, Jean-Yves, 2003, *Being Still: Reflections on an Ancient Mystical Tradition*, trans. M. S. Laird OSA, Leominster: Gracewing.

Lossky, Vladimir, 1976, *The Mystical Theology of the Eastern Church*, New York: St Vladimir's Seminary Press.

Louth, Andrew, 1981, *The Origins of the Christian Mystical Tradition: From Plato to Denys*, Oxford: Clarendon Press.

———, 1996, *Maximus the Confessor*, London: Routledge.

Luibheid, Colm, 1987, *Pseudo-Dionysius: The Complete Works*, Classics of Western Spirituality, New York: Paulist Press.

Luibheid, Colm and Norman Russell, 1982, *John Climacus: The Ladder of Divine Ascent*, Classics of Western Spirituality, New York: Paulist Press.

Mack, John, 1999, *Ascending the Heights: A Layman's Guide to* The Ladder of Divine Ascent, Ben Lomond, CA: Conciliar Press.

Maloney, George A., SJ, 1992, *Pseudo-Macarius: The Fifty Spiritual Homilies and the Great Letter*, Classics of Western Spirituality, New York: Paulist Press.

———, 1997, *Gold, Frankincense, and Myrrh: An Introduction to Eastern Christian Spirituality*, New York: Crossroad Publishing Company.

Markides, Kyriacos C., 2001, *The Mountain of Silence: A Search for Orthodox Spirituality*, New York: Image/Doubleday.

———, 2005, *Gifts of the Desert: The Forgotten Path of Christian Spirituality*, New York: Doubleday.

Mathewes-Green, Frederica, 1997, *Facing East: A Pilgrim's Journey into the Mysteries of Orthodoxy*, New York: HarperOne.

———, 2009, *The Jesus Prayer: The Ancient Desert Prayer that Tunes the Heart to God*, Brewster: Paraclete Press.

Matthew the Poor (Father Matta El-Meskeen), 2003, *Orthodox Prayer Life: The Interior Way*, translated in the Monastery of St Macarius the Great, Wadi El-Natroun, Egypt, Crestwood, NY: St Vladimir's Seminary Press.

Matus, Thomas, 2010, *Yoga and the Jesus Prayer*, Winchester: O Books.

Mayes, Andrew D., 2021, *Diving for Pearls: Exploring the Depths of Prayer with Isaac the Syrian*, Collegeville, MN: Liturgical Press.

McGuckin, John Anthony, 2001, *Standing in God's Holy Fire: The Byzantine Tradition*, Traditions of Christian Spirituality Series, London: Darton, Longman & Todd.

——— (ed.), 2014, *The Concise Encyclopedia of Orthodox Christianity*, Chichester: John Wiley & Sons.

———, 2017, 'The Prayer of the Heart in Patristic & Early Byzantine Tradition' in *Illumined in the Spirit: Studies in Orthodox Spirituality*, Volume 3 of Collected Studies, New York: St Vladimir's Seminary Press, pp. 59–102.

McVey, Kathleen E., 1989, *Ephraim the Syrian: Hymns*, Classics of Western Spirituality, New York: Paulist Press.

Merrill, Christopher, 2004, *Journey to the Holy Mountain: Meditations on Mount Athos*, London: HarperCollins.

Merton, Thomas, 1961/1974, *The Wisdom of the Desert: Sayings from the Desert Fathers of the Fourth Century*, London: Sheldon Press.

Meyendorff, John (ed.), and Nicholas Gendle (trans.), 1983, *Gregory Palamas—The Triads*, Classics of Western Spirituality, Mahwah, NJ: Paulist Press.

———, 1998, *A Study of Gregory Palamas*, trans. George Lawrence, 2nd edn, Crestwood, NY: St Vladimir's Seminary Press.

Meyer, Robert T., 1964, *Palladius: The Lausiac History*, Ancient Christian Writers, New York: Paulist Press.

Middleton, H., 2003, *Precious Vessels of the Holy Spirit: The Lives and Counsels of Contemporary Elders of Greece*, Thessalonica: Protecting Veil Press.

A Monk of Mount Athos, 2014, *The Watchful Mind: Teachings on the Prayer of the Heart*, trans. George Dokos, New York: St Vladimir's Seminary Press.

Moore, Archimandrite Lazarus, 1959, *St John Climacus: The Ladder of Divine Ascent*, London: Faber and Faber.

Paisios, Elder of Mount Athos, 2011, *Spiritual Counsels Volume 1: With Pain and Love for Contemporary Man*, revd 3rd edn, Thessaloniki: Holy Monastery 'Evangelist John the Theologian'.

———, 2010, *Spiritual Counsels Volume 2: Spiritual Awakening*, Thessaloniki: Holy Monastery 'Evangelist John the Theologian.'

Palmer, G. E. H., Philip Sherrard and Kallistos Ware, 1979, 1981, 1984, 1995, 2023, *The Philokalia: The Complete Text, compiled by St Nikodimos of the Holy Mountain and St Makarios of Corinth*, Five Volumes, London: Faber.

Pennington, Basil, OCSO, 1979, *O Holy Mountain: Journal of a Retreat on Mount Athos*, London: Geoffrey Chapman.

Plested, Marcus, 2004, *The Macarian Legacy: The Place of Macarius-Symeon in the Eastern Christian Tradition*, Oxford Theological Monographs, Oxford: Oxford University Press.

———, 2015, 'The Ascetic Tradition' in Pauline Allen and Bronwen Neil, *The Oxford Handbook of Maximus the Confessor*, Oxford: Oxford University Press, pp. 164–76.

Porphyrios, 2005, *Wounded by Love: The Life and the Wisdom of Saint Porphyrios*, edited from an archive of notes and recordings by the Sisters of the Holy Convent of Chrysopigi, Greece, Limni, Evia: Denise Harvey (publisher).

Pseudo-Athanasius, 2003, *The Life & Regimen of the Blessed & Holy Syncletica, Part 1, The Translation*, by Elizabeth Bryson Bongie, Eugene, OR: Wipf & Stock.

Ramelli, Ilaria L. E., 2015, *Evagrius, Kephalaia Gnostica: A New Translation of the Unreformed Text from the Syriac*, Atlanta, GA: Society of Biblical Literature Press.

Ramon, Brother and Simon Barrington-Ward, 2001, *Praying the Jesus Prayer Together*, Oxford: The Bible Reading Fellowship.

Rousseau, Philip, 1999, *Pachomius: The Making of a Community in Fourth-Century Egypt*, Berkeley, CA: University of California Press.

Russell, Norman, 2004, *The Doctrine of Deification in the Greek Patristic Tradition*, Oxford: Oxford University Press.

Rutherford, Janet Elaine, 2000, *One Hundred Practical Texts of Perception and Spiritual Discernment from Diadochos of Photike*, Belfast Byzantine Texts and Translations, 8, Belfast: Belfast Byzantine Enterprises.

Schaffer, Mary, 2001, *The Life & Regimen of the Blessed & Holy Syncletica, Part Two: A Study of the Life*, Eugene, OR: Wipf & Stock.

Simones, Fr Constantine (Charles) J., 2013, *Miraculous Occurrences and Counsels of Elder Porphyrios*, Milessi: The Transfiguration of the Saviour Publications.

Sinkewicz, Robert E. (trans.), 2003, *Evagrius of Pontus: The Greek Ascetic Corpus*, Oxford: Oxford University Press.

Speake, Graham, 2002, *Mount Athos: Renewal in Paradise*, New Haven, CT: Yale University Press.

Spidlík, Tomás, SJ, 1986, *The Spirituality of the Christian East: A Systematic Handbook*, trans. Anthony P. Gythiel, Collegeville, MN: Cistercian Publications.

Stethatos, Niketas, 2013, *The Life of Saint Symeon the New Theologian*, trans. Richard P. H. Greenfield, Dumbarton Oaks Medieval Library, Cambridge MA: Harvard University Press.

Swan, Laura, 2001, *The Forgotten Desert Mothers: Sayings, Lives and Stories of Early Christian Women*, New York: Paulist Press.

Thunberg, Lars, 1995, *Microcosm and Mediator: The Theological Anthropology of Maximus the Confessor*, 2nd edn, Chicago, IL: Open Court.

Turner H. J. M., 2009 (ed. and trans.), *The Epistles of St Simeon the New Theologian*, Oxford Early Christian Texts, Oxford: Oxford University Press.

Van Bavel, Tarsicius J., OSA, and Raymond Canning OSA, 1984, *The Rule of Saint Augustine*, London: Darton, Longman & Todd.

Vivian, Tim, 2004, *Saint Macarius the Spiritbearer: Coptic Texts Relating to Saint Macarius the Great*, New York: St Vladimir's Seminary Press.

———, 2021, *The Sayings and Stories of the Desert Fathers and Mothers, volume 1*, Collegeville, MN: Cistercian Publications.

———, 2023, *The Sayings and Stories of the Desert Fathers and Mothers, volume 2*, Collegeville, MN: Cistercian Publications.

Ward, Benedicta SLG, 1975/1984 revd edn, *The Sayings of the Desert Fathers: The Alphabetical Collection*, Collegeville, MN: Cistercian Publications.

———, 1987, *Harlots of the Desert: A Study of Repentance in Early Monastic Sources*, Cistercian Studies Series, Collegeville, MN: Cistercian Publications.

———, 2003, *The Desert Fathers: Sayings of the Early Christian Monks* [the Thematic Collection], London: Penguin Books.

Ware, Bishop Kallistos, 1974, *The Power of the Name: The Jesus Prayer in Orthodox Spirituality*, Oxford: SLG Press.

———, 1979/1995 revd edn *The Orthodox Way*, New York: St Vladimir's Seminary Press.

———, 1985, 'Ways of Contemplation and Prayer, 1. Eastern' in Bernard McGinn, John Meyendorff and Jean Leclercq (eds), *Christian Spirituality: Origins to the Twelfth Century*, New York: Crossroad, pp. 395–414.

———, 2001, *The Inner Kingdom, Volume 1 of the Collected Works*, New York: St Vladimir's Seminary Press.

White, Carolinne, 2009, *Early Christian Lives*, London: Penguin Books.

Wilkinson, John, 1971, *Egeria's Travels*, London: SPCK.
Williams, Rowan, 2004, *Silence and Honey Cakes: The Wisdom of the Desert*, London: Lion Hudson.
———, 2024, *Passions of the Soul*, London: Bloomsbury Continuum.